I0535271

Pamphlets by Daniel Defoe

Volume II

Daniel Defoe is most well-known for his classic novels *Robinson Crusoe* and *Moll Flanders*. Born around 1660, he was also a journalist, a pamphleteer, a businessman, a spy. His life was long and colourful, and the breadth of his work, still highly regarded, is infused with similar vigour.

It is said that only the bible has been printed in more languages than Robinson Crusoe. Defoe is also noted for being one of the earliest proponents of the novel. He was extremely prolific and a very versatile writer, producing several hundred books, pamphlets, and journals on various topics including politics, crime, religion, marriage, psychology and the supernatural. He was also a pioneer of economic journalism though was made bankrupt on more on one occasion and usually mired in debt.

In later life Defoe was often most seen on Sundays when bailiffs and the like could legally make no move on him. Allegedly it was whilst hiding from creditors that he died on April 24th, 1731. He was interred in Bunhill Fields, London.

Index of Contents

THE LAY-MAN'S SERMON UPON THE LATE STORM

Held forth at an Honest Coffee-House-Conventicle. Not so much a Jest as 'tis thought to be.

NAHUM. I. III

The Lord has his way in the Whirle-Wind and in the Storm, and the Clouds are the Dust of his Feet.

This Text is not chosen more for the Suitableness to the present Callamity, which has been the Portion of this Place, than for the aptness of the Circumstances, 'twas spoken of God going to Chastise, a Powerful, Populous, Wealthy and most reprobate City.

Nineveh was the Seat of a mighty Empire, a Wealthy Encreasing People, Opulent in Trade, Flourishing in Power and Proud in Proportion.

The Prophet does not seem to deliver these words, to the Ninevites, to convince them, or encline them to consider their own Circumstances and repent, but he seems to speak, it to the Israelites inviteing them to Triumph and Insult over the Heathen adversary, by setting forth the Power of their God, in the most exalted Terms.

And that this is a just Exposition of this Text, seems plain from the words Imediately going before, the Lord is slow to Anger, and Great in Power and will not at all acquit the wicked. These words could have no Connexion with the Text, tho' they are joyn'd with them in the same Verse, if it were not meant of his being slow to Anger, to his own People, and Terrible to the Heathen World, and this being spoken as an Expression of his being not easily provoked as to his Church, the Subsequent part of the Verse tells them how his power and Vengance is matter of particular Satisfaction to his People as being exercis'd in Revenging the affront put upon his Glory by his Enemies, God is Jealous, and the Lord Revengeth, the Lord Revengeth and is Furious, the Lord will take Vengeance on his adversaries and he reserveth wrath for his Enemies. Tis plain this is meant of his Enemies, but as if brought in with a Parenthesis, tis spoken for the comfort of his Church, the Lord is slow to Anger as to them, and to lift up their hearts in a further confidence that their Enemies are all in his hand, he goes on discribing the Terrors of his Judgement.

The Lord has his way in the Whirl-wind and in the Storm, and the Clouds are the Dust of his Feet. Eloquent Flourishes upon the Omnipotence of God.

The short Exposition I shall make of the words, Tends only to remind us that the Whirl-wind and Storm which are here made use of, to express the Magnipotent power of God are acted by his Direction, he has his way in them, it may note indeed the Invisible secrecy and swiftness of his providences, but to avoid long Paraphrases, I confine my self to my own Construction, as that which, as it is a just inference from the matter of the Text, so 'tis most suitable to the design of this discourse.

And as this Sermon may be a little Immethodical, because I purpose to make it almost all Aplication so I shall advance some Conclusions from the Premises which I lay down, as the Geneuine sence of the Words.

1. The Omnipotence of God gives Christians sufficient ground to Insult their Enemies, wherefore do the Heathen Mock thy People and say unto them where is now your God? Behold our God is in the Heavens, and doeth whatsoever he pleaseth; as the Prophet Elija, Banter'd the Heathen Priest of Baal, with the Impotence of their Gods, Cry aloud for he is a God, either he is talking or he Is Pursuing, or he is in a Journey, or Peradventure he Sleepeth and must be awakned, so he insulted them about the power of the true God, let it be known O Lord says he this day that thou art God in Israel.

2. As God in all the works of his Providence, makes use of the subserviency of means, so the whole Creation is Subordinate to the Execution of his Divine will, the Clouds are the Dust of his Feet and he rides upon the Wings of the Wind, the most Powerful Elements are so subjected to his almighty power that the Clouds are but as Dust under his feet, tis as easy for him to Govern and mannage them; as it is for a man to shake off the Dust from his feet, or he can as easily subdue the fury of them as a man Tramples the Dust, they are small and Triffling things, in his Eyes.

3. The ways of God are unsearchable, the Methods of his Providence are secret and powerfull; his way is in the Whirle-wind, and in the Storm, tis invisible and iresistible, invisible as the Wind, and iresistible as the Storm.

But waving these and abundance more usefull observations which might be justly drawn from so rich a Text, I shall proceed upon one which tho' it favours something more of private authority, and I have not so Authentick Opinion of the Learned Commentators, on my side, yet I shall endeavour not to Merit much Censure, in the Improvement of it, even from those who perhaps may not joyn with me in the Exposition.

According therefore to my own private opinion of these words; I shall for the present occasion only Paraphrase them thus, that the Lord has a way or an end in the Whirle-wind, and in the Storm, nor is this a very unusual Method of expressing things in Scripture, where the way is Exprest, to signify the design, or end of a thing.

And from this Exposition I advance this head.

That as God by his power Governs the elements, so in all their Extraordinary Motions, they are in a Perticular manner acted by his Soveraignity. And,

2. When the Creation is put into any Violent or Supernatural Agitation, God has always some Extraordinary thing to bring to pass, he has a meaning in all the Remarkables of Nature.

3. We ought dilligently to observe the extraordinary actings of Providence, in order to discover and Deprecate the displeasure of Almighty God, Providences are never Dumb, and if we can not discern the signals of his Anger, we must be very blind. The Voice of his Judgements is heard in the Voice of Nature, and if we make our selves Deaf, he is pleas'd to make them speak the Louder, to awaken the stupifyed sences, and startle the World, which seem'd rather Amus'd than Amas'd, with the common Course of things. This I take to be some of the true meaning of the way of God, in the Whirle-wind, and in the Storm.

The design of this Discourse therefore, is to put the Nation in general upon proper Resolutions; if we pretend to believe that there is any such thing as a Collateral Sympathy, a Communication of Circumstances, between a Nations Follies, and her Fate. Any Harmony between Merit and Mischief, between the Crimes of Men and the Vengeance of Heaven; we cannot but allow this Extra-Pulpit admonition to be just.

And let not any man Object against this being call'd a Sermon, and its being introduc'd from a Text of Scripture while the remainer of this Discourse, seems wholly Civil and Political.

If all our Measures in Civil affairs were deduc'd as Inferences from sacred Texts, I am of the Opinion the Text would be well improv'd, and Publick matters never the worse Guided.

And for this reason, tho' the Subject be not Treated, with the Gravity of a Sermon, nor in so serious a manner, as would become a Pulpit, yet it may be not the less suitable to the occasion and for the manner, it must be placed to the Authors account.

Besides the Title I think has provided for the Method and If so he that expected it otherwise than it is tis his Fault, and not Mine.

The Term Sermon which is but Sermo, a Speech, may Justify all the Novelty of my Method if those who find fault please to give themselves leave to allow it, and since it has never profain'd the Pulpit, I believe the Text will receive no Prejudice by it, I wish every Sermon equally Improv'd.

And what tho' your Humble Servant be no Man of the Text; if he be a Man of Honesty, he may have a hand in making you all Men of Application.

In publick Callamities, every Circumstance is a Sermon, and every thing we see a Preacher.

The trembling Habitations of an Unthinking People Preach to us, and might have made any Nation in the World tremble but us; when we were rock'd out of our Sleep as Children are Rock'd into it; and when the terrible Hand of Soveraign Power rock'd many a Wretch from one Sleep to another, and made a Grave of the Bed, without the Ceremony of waking in the Passage.

The shatter'd Palaces of our Princes Preach to us, and tell us aloud, that without respect to Dignity, he is able to put that Dreadful Text in Execution; That if a Nation does wickedly they shall be destroy'd both they and their King.

The fallen Oaks, which stood before to tell us they were the longest liv'd of all God's Creatures, Preach to us, and tell us that the most towring object of humane Beauty and strength must lye humble and prostrate, when he is pleased to give a Check to that Splendor which was deriv'd from his Power.

The Wrecks of our Navies and Fleets Preach to us, that 'tis in vain we pretend to be Wall'd about by the Ocean, and ride Masters of the Sea: And that, if he who bestow'd that Scituation upon us thinks fit, he can make that Element which has been our Strength, and the Encreaser of our Wealth, be the Grave of our Treasure, and the Enemy of our Commerce; he can put it into so violent Agitation, by the blast of his Mouth, that all our Defence and the Naval Strength we have vallued our selves so much upon, shall at once be swallow'd up in the Mouth of our Friend the Sea; and we shall find our Destruction in the very thing from which we expected our Defence.

Our Seamen and Soldiers, whose Dead Bodies Embrace the English Shores, Preach aloud to us, that whenever we think fit to Embark them on any Design, which Heaven approves not of, he can blast the Embrio, and devour those People whose Hands are lifted up against Justice and Right.

Also they Preach to us, Not to build our hopes of Success upon the multitude of Ships or Men, who are thus easily reduc'd, and the Strength of a whole Nation brought to Ruine in a Moment.

These are the Monitors of our Missfortunes, and some of these admonitions would be well preach'd from the Mouths of those whose Tallent as well as Office gives them reason to do it, and us to expect it.

But since the Sons of the Prophets have not yet thought it proper to enter very far into this Matter, not doubting but they will in due time find it as suitable to their Inclination as 'tis to their Duty,

In the mean time let us see if no uncommon Application may be made of so uncommon a Circumstance.

First, 'tis matter of wonder that any Man can be so senceless, as to suppose there is nothing extraordinary in so signal an Instance of a Supream Power; but 'tis much more remarkable that those who have Religion enough to own it a Judgment, are yet at a loss how to appropriate it's signification.

Every one thinks it to be a Judgment upon the Person or Parties they see touch'd with it. W— the Carpenter was knock'd on the head with a Stack of Chimneys, and his Wife saved; all the Neighbours cried out 'twas a Judgment upon him for keeping a Whore; but if Stacks of Chimnies were to have fallen on the Heads of all that keep Whores, Miserere Dei.

S— was kill'd by the like Accident, and he must be singl'd out for Extortion; But think ye that he was a Sinner above all the Gallileans?

The Jacobites and Non-Jurants shall rise up in Judgment against this Generation, and shall condemn them, for they tell us, this Storm is a Judgment on the whole Nation, for Excluding their Lawful Soveraign, and Abjuring his Posterity: Upon this head they have been preaching up Repentance, and Humiliation to us; and some of them are willing to reduce all to a very practical Exhortation, and tell us, we ought to look upon it as a Loud Call to Restore the Right Owner (as they call him) to the Possession of his own again; that is, in short, to rebel against a Mild, Gentle, Just and Protestant Queen, and call in the Popish Posterity of an abdicated Tyrant.

These Gentlemen are Men of Uses and Application, and know very well how to make an Advantage of God's Judgments, when they serve their turn.

The Whigs and Occasional Conformists shall rise up in Judgment against this Generation; for they are sensible of the present severe Stroke of Providence, and think 'tis a mark of Heavens Displeasure upon the Nation, for the violent methods made use of by some People against them, for their Religion, contrary to their Native Right, and the Liberty of their Consciences.

Some think a general Blast follows all the Endeavours of this Nation against the Common Enemy, for their slighting and reproaching the Glorious Memory of the late King William, whose Gallant Endeavours for the general good of Europe, and of England in particular, were Treacherously thwarted and disappointed while he was alive, and are Basely and Scandalously undervalued and slighted now he is Dead; and of this sort I confess my self enclined to be one.

From these general Observations we may descend to particulars, and every one judges according to their own Fancy.

Some will have it, that the Slaughter and Destruction among the Fleet, is a Judgment upon them, for going into the Streights, and coming home again without doing any business; but those forget, that if they did all they were ordered to do, the Fault lies in those who sent them, and not in they that went.

Some will have the Damage among the Colliers to be a Judgment, upon those who have Engross'd the Trade, and made the Poor pay so dear for Coals; not enquiring whether those Engrossers of the Coals are not left safe on Shore, while the poor Seamen are drown'd, who know nothing of the matter.

'Tis plain to me, who ever are Punish'd by the Storm, we that are left have a share in the Judgment, and a Trebble concern in the Cause.

If it could be said that those who are destroy'd, or who have suffered the loss of Lives, Limbs or Goods, were the only People who gave any occasion to the Divine Justice thus severely to Revenge it self, then all admonition to the rest of Mankind would be useless, any farther than it directed them to be Cautious how they provoked him in like manner; but have we not all had a hand in the general provocation, though not an equal share in the general Calamity.

Sometimes the Judgements of Heaven, bear so much Analogy to the Crimes, that the Punishment points out the Offence, and 'tis easy to distinguish what it is the perticular hand of Justice points at.

And if we will seek for a Perticular case, in which Heaven seems to have singled out this way of Punishment on the Nation, as best proportion'd to the general National Crime we are all guilty of? what seems more Rational than to Judge that tis a severe Animadversion upon the Feuds and Storms of parties kept up among us in this Nation, with such unnatural Heat, and such unaccountable Fury, that no man, who has the least Compassion for his Native Country, but must with more than Common Grief, be concerned for it, since unless some speedy course be taken to bring a general Composure upon the minds of Men, the general ruin seems Inevitable.

If the matters in Debate were of Extraordinary Consequence, there might be some pretence for Espousing contrary parties with unusual heat; but while the difference lies in small, and, in some cases, indifferent things, tis a most inexcusable Madness that the Feuds shou'd be run up so high, that all manner of Charity should Perish and be lost among us.

We have had an Extraordinary Bustle in the World about Moderation, and all Parties pretend to it, and now we are as busy about Peace, and every one lays in a Loud Claim to it.

I have seen, with some regret, the strange Mysterious Management of this Age about Moderation, and tho' some late Authors have Published that Moderation is a Vertue, It begins to be a question whether it is or no.

I wish some Body would make enquiry after the occasion that has brought this Blessed Word into so much Contempt in the World; tis very hard that a word expressive of the most Glorious Principle in the World, should become the Brand of reproach, and a Badge of Infamy to Parties; be a Nick-name it self, and be Nick-nam'd on every side; and that at a time when the Vertue it self, is perhaps the only thing left in the World, that can preserve this Nation from Destruction.

'Tis too unhappy for England, that Men of immoderate Principles are so powerfull as they are. Let the Party be which it will, tis Destruction even to themselves, to run up all their Nicetles and all their Scruples to the Extremes. Every Dispute becomes a Feud, every Spark a Flame, every word a Blow, every Blow, a Civil-War, and by this Intestine Confusion of Principles, Backt with the Passion and Fury of Men, this unhappy Nation is Subdivided into an Infinite Number of Parties, Factions, Intrests and seperate Opinions.

Every Man being thus bent upon the propagation of his own Notion, for want of this healing Spirit of Moderation, falls foul upon his Neighbour because he has not the same Heat, and if he finds him better Temper'd than himself, if he finds him less Violent, less Furious, than himself, he is Imediately Branded with the Scandal of Moderation.

Since then the Change of times has made this Practice, which in its very Nature is a Foundation of Vertue, become a Crime, Let us examine who are, and who are not Guilty of it.

For the Negatives of this Vice of Moderation they are something Easier to be discover'd than ordinary, both in Principles and in Practice; and, without the Scandal of a Censorious Writer, I may be allowed to say all the following Instances may stand clear of this Crime.

1. If Mr. Sachaverell, with his Bloody Flag, and Banner of Defiance, were Indicted for Moderation, I verily believe no Jury would bring him in Guilty.

2. If Dr. J—ne, Author of the Character of a Low-Churchman, Mr. — Author of the New Association, if a famous Bishop who told us, 'twould never be well with England till all the Dissenters were serv'd like the Hugonots in France, if any of these were Indicted for Moderation, they might safely plead not Guilty.

3. If Sir John Friend and Sir William Parkins, had been only accus'd for Moderation, they had never been Hanged, nor Collyer and Cook had never absolv'd them at the Gallows without Repentance.

4. If he were Hang'd for Moderation, who ask'd the Question, whether if the Play-house in Dorset-Garden, were let for a Meeting-house, 'twould not do more harm than tis like to do as a Theatre, he would certainly Dye Innocently.

5. If Fuller had been Voted an Incorrigible Rogue only for the Vice of Moderation, I should have thought the House of Commons had done him wrong.

6. If the Councellors of the late King, such as Father P—, my Lord S— and all those that betray'd their Master, by hurrying on his ruin and their own. If those Gentlemen were Charged with Moderation, I doubt we should wrong them.

7. If some of the Members of our Late Convocation shou'd be accused for Moderation, I believe it might be no Difficult task to Vindicate them.

8. If this Crime should be Charged higher than we dare to mention, I am perswaded some Persons of Note would think themselves abused.

9. In short all those Gentlemen, by whatsoever Names or Titles Distinguish'd, who repine at the Settlement, who reproach the Tolleration, and who Blame the Queen for her promises of Maintaining it, these abhor the thoughts of this Scandalous Crime of Moderation, and are as Innocent of it as the Child unborne.

10. Tis the Opinion of some People, That there are some of our beloved Friends in Scotland, may be Vindicated in this case, nay others are of the Opinion, tis not a National Crime in that Country, that is, 'tis not a sin the Scots are much adicted to.

11. Lastly, Take our English Clergy in general, some are ready to say they have no great cause of Repentance for the sin of Moderation.

On the other hand, some People have so home a Charge of this Error laid upon them, that 'twill be very hard to clear themselves of it, and I am afraid they would be brought in Guilty by a Jury, almost without going away from the Bar. as,

1. Our Observator, they say, is Guilty of Moderation, with Relation to his Wit, and Especially as concerning his good Manners; I hope he wont be prosecuted for it the next Sessions, if he should, I doubt, 'twill go hard with him.

2. If our News-writers should be Indited for Moderation, as to Truth of Fact, I would advise them to plead Guilty, and throw themselves upon the Mercy of the Court.

3. Some of our Captains, they say, are addicted to Fight but Moderately; I hope all the rest wont be Infected, but I know not what to say to it.

4. Some of our Lawyers are apt to be very Moderate in their Justice, but being well read in the Law are cunning enough to keep off an Indictment, so there is no fear of them.

5. Some of our General Receivers, when they got the Publick Money in their hands, were apt to be very Moderate in paying it out again.

6. Some have been very Moderate in giving in their accounts too, as may appear in former Reigns, and perhaps in time to come too.

Some Moderately Wise, some Moderatly Honest, but most Immoderately adicted to think themselves Both.

Tho' I might be a little more serious upon the matter, yet this way of talking is not so much a Jest neither as it looks like; and has its Moral, in it self, which a Wise man may see, and for the Fool tis no matter whether he does or no. Custome has prevailed upon us to such a degree, that almost in every part the very Practice seem a Scandal, and the Word passes for a Reproach.

To say, among the Sons of Levy, such a man is a Moderate Church-man is to say he is no Church-man, and some of our present Bishops from the Practice of Moderation have been boldly call'd Presbiterians in the Pamphlets of our less Moderate writers.

In short, 'tis hard to find any party or profession of Men among us, that care for the Title; and those who but Moderately espouse an Intrest, are generally suspected by those who are of that side, as Persons Favouring their Enemies.

These Moderate Men, said a Gentleman whose Gown and Band had given us reason to expect better Language, they will Ruin the Church, this Damn'd Moderation, says he, spoils all, we should deal well enough with the Dissenters, if it were not for these men of Moderation, they are worse than Dissenters, for they seem to be among us, and yet wont Joyn heartily to do the Work.

Moderation seems to be cast off on every side, and is used as a Badge of reproach in every Class, or degree of Men in the World.

In the Church of England, 'tis call'd Low-Church.

In the Court, 'tis call'd Whiggism.

In the Dissenters, 'tis call'd Occasional Conformity.

In Parties, 'tis call'd Trimming.

In Religion, 'tis call'd Latitudinarian.

In Opinion, 'tis call'd Indifference,

In the Church of Scotland, 'tis call'd Prelacy.

While Moderation of principles seems thus the general Sin of Parties, Let them consider whether Heaven it self has not declar'd War against us all on this Head, and fill'd us with immoderate Judgements.

Where's all our prospect of success Abroad, or prosperity at home? Since our late Thanksgiveing for Victories, how has Heaven Treated us, but like a Nation, that being puff'd up and exalted with prosperity, began to slight Forreign Judgements, and leaving Providence to Work by it self fell to making War at home with one another, as if we would prove that the Scripture was not true and that a Kingdom might stand tho' it were divided against it self.

How has Heaven declar'd that he is resolv'd not to bless this immoderate Generation? How has all their Measures been disappointed both abroad and at home, all their designes been blasted, and the Anger of Heaven so remarkably bent against them, that even the little success we have had, has been prescrib'd by Providence to those few hands who Act from Principles of Honesty and Temper, as if God did thereby point out to us who they are he delights to bless.

The D— of M— is a Whig say some of our People who Hate all Moderation, he is so Dutchify'd, we shall never have any Good of him, why that may be, but yet you see there is not one Article of our Conduct has succeeded but what has been under his Mannagement.

And Heaven has declar'd so Eminently against all other Branches of our Affaires, that I wish I am mistaken when I say 'tis plain either he seems to mislike the Cause or the Persons employ'd, and that however severe he was pleas'd to Anminadvert upon the Publick affaires in the late Violent Tempest, it seems that for all this his Anger is not turned away but his hand is Stretched out still.

But what has a Sermon to do to enquire, may some say, and if it had, how shall it make appear whether God is displeased with our designs or the Persons employed, with the cause or the Carryers of it on.

As to the cause, all men are Judges of the Justice of it, and all men know the Foot of the present Confederacy, at least our part must be Just as it is to Maintain our just Rights, Liberty, Trade and Religion.

It must then be the Persons, the R—s, the Sir G—s, G—ns, the R—ks of this War; that Heaven is resolv'd shall not be the men, whom he will honour with the Deliverance of his People.

All wise Princes in the World have made it a constant Maxim in their Governments, that when any of their great Generals prove Unfortunate, tho' never so Wise, they lay them by, as Persons that God does not think fit to bless with success, and 'tis not needful to examine whether it were not their fault, but to be Unfortunate is to be told from Heaven, that such a one is not the Man, and a Nation ought to understand it so.

But sure when Heaven Singles men out by Crossing their attempts and Marks them for unfortunate, and we can give our selves good reasons why they are thus Mark'd by the Divine displeasure; when we can see their false steps, their General designs against God and their Countries Intrests, 'tis high time then for those who sit at the Helm of Government, to Change hands and put their affaires into such Persons Conduct, against whom Heaven has not declar'd so plainly its Displeasure, nor the Nation its Dislike.

Why shou'd the Queen be desir'd to Chain down her own Happiness and the Nations Interest, to the Missfortune of a few Men. Perhaps God may Bless the Fleet under one Admiral, when he will not under another. I know nothing against Admiral Callemburgh, he may be an Honest and worthy-man, and ready enough to Fight for the cause, for indeed most of the Dutch Captains of Ships are so, but since Heaven has now 'twice refus'd to let him go, and driven him back again, if I were the Governour of his Masters affairs, he should not be sent a Third time, least we should seem obstinately to Employ somebody that God himself had declar'd against and had three times from Heaven forbid to go.

I hope no Body will Construe this to be a Personal Satyr upon Myn Heer Callemburgh, But take it among ye, let it go, where it Fitts best.

If these are not the Generation of Men that must do the Nations business, then 'tis plain our Deliverance will never be wrought while they are employ'd; If God will not bless them he will never bless us till they are dismist.

I doubt not we shall be deliver'd, and this Nation shall yet Triumph over her Enemies; but while wrong Instruments are Employ'd the Work will be delay'd. God would have a House built him But David was not the Man and therefore the Work was put off till Solomon was in the Throne.

God would have Israel go into the Land of Canaan and possess it, but those Generals and those Captains were not the Men; Moses and Aaron, and the great Men of the Camp were not such as God approv'd off and therefore Israel could not go over Joardan till they had laid their Bones in the Wilderness.

England is hardly ever to pass over the Jourdan before her, till these Immoderate Men of Strife and Storms are laid by.

If any man ask me why these men shou'd not perfect the Nation Peace as well as other men? I do not say which Men nor who, but let them be who the enquirer please, I answer the Question, with a question How shou'd men of no Moderaion bring us to Peace.

How shou'd Men of strife bring us Peace and Union: Contraries may Illustrate but Contraries never Incorporate; Men of Temper, are the safe men for this Nation. Men of heat are fit to Embroil it, but not to Cure it: they are something like our Sea Surgeons who fly to Amputation of Members upon every slight Fracture, when a more proper Application would effect the Cure and save the Joynt.

'Tis an ill sign especially for England when Wars abroad wont make us Friends at home. Foreign dangers us'd to Unite us from whence Queen Elizabeth, has been said to leave this Character of the Nation behind her, that they were much easier to be Govern'd in a time of War than in Peace.

But when This, which us'd to be the only Cure of all our diseases, fails us, 'tis a sign the Distemper is Grown very strong, and there is some more than usual Room for despair.

The only Way left the Nation is to obtain from those in power, that Moderation may cease being the pretence and be really the practice.

It would be well all men would at least be Occasional Conformists, to this Extraordinary principle; and when there is such a Loud call to Peace both from Heaven and from the Throne, they would do well to consider who are the Men of Peace and who are not: For certainly those Immoderate Gentlemen, who slight the Proposals for a general Union of Charity, cannot pretend to be Friends to the present Intrest of their Native Country.

These men, 'tis true, Cry out of the danger of the Church, but can they make it appear that the Church is in any danger from Moderation and Temper; can they pretend that there is no way to secure her, but by pulling down all that differ with them, no way to save her but by the ruin of her Protestant Brethren; there are Thousands of Loyal honest Church-men, who are not of this mind; who believe that Moderation and Charity to Protestant Dissenters is very Consistant with the safety of the Church and with the present general Union which they Earnestly desire.

As to Persons we have nothing to say to them, but this, without pretending to prophesy, may be safely advanced, that Heaven it self, has Eminently declared it self against the Fury and Immoderate Zeal of those Gentlemen, and told us as plainly as possible, unless we would Expect a Voice from on high, that he neither Has nor Designs to bless this Generation nor their proceedings.

When ever our rulers think fit to see it, and to employ the Men and the Methods which Heaven approves, then we may expect success from abroad, Peace at home, prosperity in Trade, Victory in War, plenty in the Field, Mild and Comfortable Seasons, Calm Air, Smooth Seas, and safe Habitations.

Till then we are to expect our Houses Blown down, our Pallaces Shatter'd, our Voyages broken, our Navys Ship-wreck'd, our Saylors Drown'd, our Confedrates Beaten, our Trade ruin'd, our Money spent and our Enemies encreased.

The Grand dispute in this Quarrelsome Age, is against our Brethren who Dissent from the Church; and from what principle do we act? it is not safe say they to let any of them be entrusted in the Government, that is, it is not profitable to let any Body enjoy great Places but themselves.

This is the Bottom of the pretence, as to the safety of it. These are the People who Cry out of the Danger from the Dissenters, but are not concerned at our Danger from the French; that are frighted at the Dissenters who as they pretend grow too Formidable for the Church, but are not disturb'd at the Threatning Growth of a Conquering Popish Enemy; that Deprecate the Clouds of Whiggism and Phanaticism, but apprehend nothing of the Black Clouds of God's Threatning Judgements, which plainly tell them if they would suffer themselves to think, that there is somthing in the general practice of the Nation which does not please him, and for which the hand of his Judgements is extended against us.

These are strange dull-sighted men, whose Intrest stands so directly between them and their understanding that they can see nothing but what that represents to them; God may Thunder from Heaven with Storms upon Storms, Ruin our Fleets, Drown our Sailors and Blow us back from the best Contriv'd Expeditions in the World, but they will never believe the case affects them, never look into their own Conduct to see if they have not help'd to bring these heavy Strokes upon the Nation.

How many Thousands have we in England, who if the whole Navy of England had been at Stake; had rather have lost it than the Bill against Occasional Conformity; that had rather the French should have taken Landau and Beat the Prince of Hess Cassell, than the Queen should have made such a Speech for Peace and Union; that had rather the Duke of Bavaria should have taken Ausburgh, than that there should not have been some Affront put upon the House of Lords.

And if such Zealots, such Christian Furies are met with by Providence, and see both the Fleet and the Occasional Bill lost together is it not plain, what Providence meant in it. He that can not see that God from on high has Punish'd them in their own way and pointed out the Crime in the Vengeance must be more blind than usual, and must shut their Eyes against their own Consciences.

'Tis plain Heaven has suited his Punishment to the Offence, has Punish'd the Stormy Temper of this Party of Men with Storms of his Vengeance, Storms on their Navies, Storms on their Houses, Storms on their Confederates, and I question not will at last with Storms in their Consciences.

If there be any Use to be made of this matter, 'tis to excite the Nation to Spue out from among them these Men of Storms, that Peace, Love, Charity and a General Union may succeed, and God may Bless us, Return to us and delight to dwell among us, that the Favour of Heaven may Return to us, and the Queen who has heartily declared her Eyes open to this needful happiness, may enjoy the Blessing of Wise Counsellors and Faithful Servants, that Constant Victory may Crown all our Enterprizes, and the General Peace of Europe may be Established.

If any one can tell us a way to bring all these Blessed ends to pass, without a General Peace of Parties and Interests at home, he is Wellcome to do it, for I profess It is hid from my Eyes.

A SHORT NARRATIVE OF THE LIFE AND ACTIONS OF HIS GRACE JOHN, DUKE OF MARLBOROUGH

Seeing the Press is open, and every body dares Write and Publish what he pleases, and Persons of the highest Honour and Virtue, to the great Shame and Scandal of our Country, are expos'd to the World, in base Pamphlets; and according to the Malice or Misunderstanding of the Authors, are represented to the World unworthy of the Favour of the Prince, as well as Obnoxious to the Common-Wealth, in which they live: It becomes every honest Man, who knows more of the Matter, to set things in a true Light, to undeceive the People, as much as he is able, that they may be no longer impos'd on by such false Reports, which in the end may prove Dangerous and Fatal.

There is nothing new, saith Solomon, under the Sun; the same Causes will always produce the same Effects; and while Mankind bear about them, the various Passions of Love and Joy, Hatred and Grief, the cunning Engineer, that stands behind the Curtain, will influence and work these Passions according to his Malice, to the destruction of Persons of highest Worth.

I shall therefore give a short Narrative of the Actions of the most Illustrious John Duke of Marlborough, with some Reflections on them, that People may not wonder how it comes to pass, that such a Great Captain, equal no doubt to any in all Ages, considering the Powers whom he has Oppos'd, after all his Victories, should be represented in the publick Writings of the Town, as over-Honoured and over-Paid for all his past Services, and neglected and almost forgotten in the midst of all his Triumphs, and his Name almost lost from the Mouths of those People, who for several Years last past, and not many Months since, have been fill'd with his Praises.

The first time that I had the Honour of seeing John, Earl of Marlborough, (for so I shall call him till he was created a Duke) was at a place call'd Judoigne in Brabant, where our Army was Encamp'd, I think about three Months after the late King was Crown'd. He was sent over the King's Lieutenant, with the British Forces under his Command, which could then be spared for that Service. Our united Forces were Commanded in general, by the Old Prince Waldeck.

After several Marches, we came to the Confines of Haynault, within a League of a small Town call'd Walcourt, and on St. Lewis's Day, a Saint suppos'd to be prosperous to the French Nation, their Army, Commanded by Mareschal d'Humiers, very betimes in the Morning, Marched to Attack us.

An English Colonel guarded a Pass towards the aforesaid little Town, to which the Enemy bent their Course; and being in Distress, was reliev'd by my Lord in Person, who ordred his Retreat to such an Advantage, that he flank'd the Enemy with perpetual Fire; and this was the first Cause that cool'd them in their Design of pushing our Army.

At his return, the Prince receiv'd him with a great deal of Satisfaction, and assured him that he would let the King know that he saw into the Art of a General more in one Day, than others do in a great many Years.

At the end of this Campaign, my Lord Marlborough was ordered, with half of the Forces under his Command, to Embark for Ireland; where I come to relate what he performed there: As soon as he arrived in the Harbour of Kingsale, having Landed his Forces, without the least loss of Time, Marched directly to the Fort or Citadel of that Place, which is a strong Fortification, and at that time, well provided with a good Garrison, and all things necessary for a strong Defence.

My Lord did not stand to use Forms with them, which might look like a Siege; but with a conquering Resolution, and perpetual Volleys, so terrified them, that they soon Surrendred.

And now at this Place it was where the Duke's Actions began to be Envied, and evil Reports touching his good Name and Reputation were industriously spread abroad; and I am apt to believe, such back Friends as these will hardly leave him so long as he remains in the World.

There was a Ship at that time in the said Harbour, which 'twas reported had some Money on Board for paying of the Forces in these Parts; which Ship, by some untimely Accident, was blown up and lost; and presently after it was given out by some ill People there present with my Lord, and by them sent into England to their Party, that he had gotten the Money beforehand to himself, and that the Ship was destroyed by his Contrivance; that he had vast Sums of Money in Holland, and at Venice; nay, some went farther and affirmed, that he had settled a good Fund, upon Occasion, at Constantinople: And I am sure some such like Reports and palpable Falsities are continued on him to this very Day.

And now I suppose it could not be in this Year that the strong City of Dunkirk was to be betrayed by the Governour of it, and Surrendred to some of the King's Forces.

In the next Campaign in Flanders, the Old Waldeck was severely beaten by Duke Luxembourg, at the Battle of Flerus: We were only Six Battalions of British left in Ghent, under the Command of the then Brigadier Talmach: We had Orders to march, and to join the grand Army at least a Fortnight before the Fight happened; but as we were about to march out of the City, the City Gates were shut against us by the People of that Place, because we had no Money to pay our Quarters.

Mr. Sizar, whom my Lord brought over with him the Year before, was our Pay-Master-General, and at this time was gone down into Holland to get some Money upon Credit, till our Supply was returned from England; and then I remember there was a barbarous Lie spread up and down among us, that our Money was kept in the Hands of Merchants by the contrivance of my Lord and Mr. Sizar, that they might reap such a particular Benefit, which could not be much, for the use of it.

Waldeck being beaten, the Elector of Brandenbourg, for supporting of him, was oblig'd by long Marches, to come and join us; after which, nothing more of Consequence happened this Year. And now I suppose it could not be in this Year that Dunkirk was to be given up to some party of the King's Forces; both his Majesty and my Lord Marlborough being absent from us, and we had no Marches towards that part of the Country, and good Reason for it, for we could not if we would.

I come now to our third Campaign, which was made in Flanders; and if ever Dunkirk was to be betrayed in some secret manner to the late King; and if ever the Secret thereof was reveal'd by his Majesty to the Earl of Marlborough; and if my Lord did reveal the same weighty Secret to his Wife; and if by her it was discovered to her Sister at St. Germans, and by her to the French King, it must be placed in this Year, or else it must be extra anni solisque Vias, the Lord knows when and where.

I am sure that the pretended Discovery of this same Secret hath lain hard on my Lord's Name for a great many Years; and upon most Discourses of the Affairs in Flanders, that business of Dunkirk is trump'd up against my Lord to this very Day.

For as soon as this Story was sent abroad, it flew like Lightening, and like the sham tragical Report which was put upon the Irish at the Revolution, it was scattered over all the Kingdom in an instant. The loss of Dunkirk is not to be forgotten, and 'tis fresh in the Minds of the common People, both in Town and Country; and not only the Farmers over a Pot of Ale at Market, will shake their Heads at Malbur, (for so they call him) for losing of Dunkirk; but also Gentlemen of good Rank and Condition believe it to be true, and talk of it with a great deal of Regret to this very time. I don't pretend in this Narrative to Inform the great People at Court, concerning this thing; without doubt they very well know there was no great matter in this mighty Secret; but most of it a design to Disgrace my Lord Marlborough, that he might the more easily be turn'd out of his Places at Court and in the Army: I write this to the common People only; to vindicate the Innocent, and to undeceive a good part of the Nation, who have not had an Opportunity to be better Informed.

This Summer then being our Third Campaign, the King came to the Army, and with Him my Lord Marlborough, and several other Persons of Quality: Among the rest was Count Solmes, a nigh Relation to his Majesty, and Colonel of the great Regiment of Dutch Blue Guards; and then it was after two or three Marches that my Lord was observ'd to be somewhat neglected, and his Interest in the Army to decay and cool; and upon a certain Morning, as we were in full March, a Man might judge by what then happened that it was so: For it seems the Count had ordered his Baggage and Sumpters to take Place of my Lord's, and to cut them out of the Line; of which Affront my Lord being inform'd by his Servants, soon found him out, and having caus'd his Baggage to enter the Post which was his due, with his Cane lifted up, and some hard Words in French, 'twas thought by a great many that it would end in a single Combat; but the Count thought fit to shear off, and we heard no more of it.

All this Summer was spent in a great many Marches after the French, to bring them to a Battle, but they Industriously and Artfully declin'd it. The Summer being spent, the King committed the Army again to Prince Waldeck, and went in haste to the Hague. Our Regiment was sent to Garrison at Mechlen, where came the Dutch Foot Guards to Winter also. Count Solmes, as he designed for Holland, took this City in his way, and there he assured a certain English Colonel, who not long before had been check'd by my Lord, about some Disorders in his Regiment, that the Earl of Marlborough had made his Peace with France, and in a short time he would hear, that he would be call'd to an Account for it.

When I went to England that same Winter, my Lord's Appartments were at the Cock-pit. 'Twas fine to see them full of Gentlemen and Officers of all Ranks, as they are now to be seen every Day at his Levee at St. James's; but no sooner had my Lord Sidney brought him word from the King, that His Majesty had no farther Service for him in the Court, or in the Army, but my Lord was forsaken by all his Shadows, and his House left in a profound Silence.

Now a Person of my Lord's high Posts, especially having been so eminently instrumental in the Revolution, could not be well laid aside from all his Employments, without some Reasons were given to the People for it; and in a short time the pretended Reasons were produced, and they prevailed mightily.

The first was, That at the King's Levee at the putting on of the Shirt, my Lord should speak scornfully of the Person of the King, who at the same time having made a great Spitting (for his Majesty was a long time troubled with a Consumptive Cough) that my Lord should say to some Gentlemen nigh him, that he wish'd it might be his last.

As soon as this gross Affront was made known to the King, by a certain Party, who can calumniate stoutly, and blast as well as blacken, it was in a Moment all over the Court and Town; and 'tis a wonder my Lord was not torn in Pieces.

But now to the Truth of this Matter. My Lord has been always esteem'd a nice Courtier, well guarded in his Words, and one of the most Mannerly best-bred Men of the Nation; and no Man of Sense can believe that a Man of his Character could be so Indiscreet, as to drop such Words, which would be Barbarous and Brutal from the Mouth of a Porter, much more from the Lips of a Noble-Man and a General.

The other Reason was, That through his or his Lady's Treachery or Indiscretion, the contrivance about Dunkirk was discovered to the French, or else 'tis very probable it would have been in our Possession. And now to clear this Aspersion also.

Dunkirk is suppos'd to be one of the strongest Fortresses of Europe, either by Sea or Land, the French King, by vast Labour, Art and Cost, having made it to be so, and accordingly regards it with a careful Eye, always keeping in it a good Garrison, with all manner of Plenty for the Defence of it. The next Garrisons of ours towards that Place, were Bruges, Ostend, and Newport, the nighest is Newport, a small Fortress on the Sea, and about twenty Miles from Dunkirk; we had no Marches towards any of these Places all this Campaign, neither was it known that any Detachment was sent that way, either in Summer or Winter: Scarce less than a body of Three Thousand Men would suffice to secure that City if it were to be betrayed to them; now how such a Party could march over so many Canals, Morasses, and Trenches in that low Country, some part of the Enemy's, & most part of it their Friends, unobserved, and not look'd after, especially a Royal Army of theirs being at Hand, is not easie to be conceived by any Person who understands the Business of a Soldier. 'Tis a great Hazzard, a nice Difficulty for a French Governour to betray a strong City; unless all his Officers be in the Secret, and then 'tis wonderful, if by some one or other it is not revealed, or else he has with him in the Place several good Officers, who understand the Duty as well as himself, and very probable that one or more of them may have private Instructions to have an Eye upon him, and to keep him in View. Every one that has a Command, knows his Alarm-Post, and every hour, Night and Day, the Majors, or their Aids, or some other Officers, go their Rounds upon the Walls all the Year long, in Places of so great Importance. As for the betraying of it to any Naval Forces, I suppose 'twas never thought on, unless the whole Garrison, with the Burghers, should give their Consent, and stand idly gazing on whilst the Ships were approaching: Indeed there was once a Design upon some Sea-port of this Garrison, to shake and shatter it with a Vessel, which was called for that purpose The Terrible Machine; it made a horrible Crack when it was Fired, and so the Engine and the Design vanish'd in Smoak.

But now admitting that all this was true, and that there was a Contrivance to put Dunkirk into our Hands, and the Plot was discovered, and the Governour was hang'd, (which upon strict Enquiry no one could tell whom he was, or when or where he was Executed) yet why must my Lord Marlborough, or his Lady, be the Betrayers of this weighty Secret? If it was for a good Reward, I suppose no one living can tell how, or when, or where it was paid. And what great Services my Lord has done for the French King, for a great many Years to this very Day; let the World judge.

But to put all this Matter out of doubt, our most Gracious Sovereign Lady the QUEEN, who was then Princess, was at that time the best Judge of this Untruth cast upon them; for notwithstanding the high displeasure of the Court, she always gave them Umbrage and Protection, which without doubt she would not have done, unless she was thoroughly persuaded of their Innocence.

To be short, my Lord was a true Lover of the Interest of his Country, and a true Member of the Church of England; and most Places of State and Power were in the Hands of such Persons, who seem'd to depress the Fences of the Church, and favour the Dissenters, and their Favourers the Whigs: So 'twas not thought convenient that my Lord should be admitted into their Secrets; upon which they gave him a good Name, and turned him out.

My Lord was no sooner discharged of his Places, but like the old Roman Dictator, with the same calmness of Temper he retired from the highest Business of State, to his Villa in the Country; but he shew'd himself as skilful an Husband-Man, as he had been a Soldier: But here he could not long enjoy the Quiet which he sought, but the same Malice found him here, which had turn'd him from the Court; from hence he was taken and clap'd up into the Tower, where most of Friends thought he would have lost that Head, which has since done so much good to his Queen and Country.

And thus I have shew'd how very much my Lord has been obliged to the Whigs in those Days. The Jacobites at this time were not behind hand with him in their good Wishes, but all they could do, was to Rail and call Names, and so promise their good Nature, when 'twas in their Power.

The King, who was certainly an able Judge of Men, had never time enough to be acquainted with the excellent Merits of this Noble Lord, but he was blasted by His Enemies, before his Virtues were sufficiently made known to Him.

But when several great Men, who were true Lovers of their Country, had fully inform'd his Majesty, that my Lord was always his most faithful Servant and Subject, and most willing to serve Him to the utmost of his Power; and that 'twas pity such an able Man should be laid by as useless and forgotten: My Lord was brought again to the King's nearer Conversation; and after the late Peace, as his Majesty found himself decaying in his Health, and the French King dealing more and more every Day insincerely with him, and his Allies, he chose him again his General, and his Ambassador to the States; and having brought him to Holland, that he might be fully instructed in all the necessary Affairs of both Nations, he recommended him to his Successor, our most Gracious QUEEN, as the only fit Person, whose Spirit might encounter the Genius of France, and strangle their Designs of swallowing Europe.

No sooner had our Sovereign Lady Queen ANNE mounted the Throne, but in concert with her High Allies, she proclaim'd War against France; and having created my Lord, Duke of Marlborough, she sent him her Plenepotentiary into Holland to the States, and Captain General of Her Forces; and I am sure a great many Officers who had serv'd under him in the former War, were glad to see him once more at the Head of an Army.

In the beginning of this first Year of the War, the French Army, under the Conduct of Mareschal Boufflers, was a little beforehand with us, and came into the Field stronger than ours; some Troops of the Allies having not yet join'd us. The French had coop'd up our Army under the Walls of Nimeguen, and much ado we had, by frequent Skirmishes, to hinder them from investing that considerable Frontier, at that time unprovided by the neglect of the Governour, as 'tis reported, of all warlike Necessaries for the Defence of it. A Man might then see but an indifferent Ayre in the face of our Forces: The States were under great Apprehensions, least the Enemy should penetrate into their Country; and nothing could recover them from their Fears, till his Grace, after three or four Days, had join'd our Army with some additional Troops; upon his Approach we had immediately a new Scene of Affairs; each Soldier seem'd to receive a new Life by the Cheerfulness of their Officers; and he presently assured the Deputies of the States, that the French should be no longer their bad Neighbours, but he would oblige them to March farther off that Country, and that with a Witness. They were like People in a Trance, and could hardly believe that their Affairs had receiv'd so happy a turn; accordingly we march'd, and having passed the Maes, Coasted along that side of Brabant, which lies towards that River, towards the open Country of Mastricht and Luickland, and not long after, almost in Sight of their Army, we opened that noble River, to the great Benefit of the Trade of the Country, having taken from the French the Fortresses of Stochum, of Stevenswaert, of Ruremond, and Venlo, and at last the strong Cittadel and City of Liege, with a vast quantity of Cannon and Prisoners; the French not daring to relieve any of them by venturing a Battle.

In this Campaign our General shew'd himself a true Master of his Art, having outdone the French Mareschal in every March. When he came into Holland, he was receiv'd into their Cities, as their Tutelar Angel, and their own Generals came to thank him for this happy Campaign, without any sign of Envy.

When he returned to England, he was well receiv'd by the Queen his Mistress, and with the Joy of all good People; but then there was some allay to this good Fortune, several People were heard to Grumble, that after this Manner we should not get to Paris in a long time, and a Speech was Printed, as if a Peer of the Realm had been the Author of it, with some ironical Touches on the Duke, about raising the ancient Valour of the Nation; and that 'twas unreasonable, that one Man should have a King-Key, which should open every Door in the Nation.

About this time also Pamphlets began to fly, much reflecting on the Countess of Marlborough, which I think have not ceas'd, but very much increased against her every Year, to this very Day. I never had the Honour to see that Lady, but once at the Hague; she was there with her Husband, the last time our late King was in that Country; and it was a common Report, at that Court, among a great many Gentlemen of very good Quality, that she was esteemed there among the Foreign Ladies, one of the best bred Women of her Age; and here are Ladies from most Courts of Europe, who, without doubt, are the nicest Judges: But to be sure here at home they give her Name very poor Quarters, and make her guilty of more Folly, than a Retainer to the College in Moor-Fields.

It will be too long for me to set down the particular Victories of every Campaign, and I hope no need of it; because 'tis probable they are fresh in the Memory of every good Subject. His wonderful and conquering March to the Banks of the Danube; His artful Passing the French Lines, purely owing to his own good Conduct; His Beating each one of the French Great Mareschals round in their Turns, in several well fought Battles: A People, who for an Age had bullied the rest of Europe, and had taught other Nations the Art and Tactiques of War, as well as their Modes and Language: Their Captiv'd Generals and Conquered Towns, perhaps the Strongest in the Universe, demonstrate not only his Wisdom, Skill and Conduct, but also his surmounting Courage, and unwearied Labour.

And now at first View a Man might wonder how it should come to pass that such a Renown'd General, after so many Signal Services, and great Actions, for the good of his Country, should be so undervalued and slighted at his return home from the very middle of his Labours, by any one who pretends to value the good of his Nation: But this is no new Thing, all the Histories of the World are full of Examples to this purpose, and most of them of Men of War and Great Captains.

Sir Walter Raleigh has mustered up a long Roll of Glorious Sufferers, from the most ancient to his own Times; and in the Condition in which he then was, might have brought in himself for a remarkable Sharer. For the most eminent Virtues are but as so many fair Marks set up on high for Envy to shoot at with her poysonous Darts, and in all States, 'tis sometimes dangerous to be Great and Good, for cunning Envy is often very strong, and when once its Devices are effectually spread in the Mouths of the Multitude, will produce a Blast able to blow down the most lofty Cedar: 'Tis therefore for the good of the common People of the Nation, that I shall let them see the scandalous Reflections which are scattered abroad on the Honour of the Duke of Marlborough; and when I have shewn to any rational Man that they are all False, Unreasonable, and Malicious, I have my End.

The first Scandal that is put abroad upon his Grace is this: That he has avoided several Opportunities of Fighting, not considering the great burden of Taxes that lies upon the Nation, because the War should be continued longer, whereby he may increase his Riches, and keep up his Power. Now how false this Report is, will easily appear.

For the Business of Peace and War does not depend on a General: 'Tis the Business of his Monarch, who best knows the proper times for such Treaties. Other Princes are concern'd in the War, as well as ours, and their Subjects are as desirous of Peace as any of us can be, yet this Peace can't well be obtain'd without a joint Consent; but if the Enemy against whom we Fight, will not come to any terms of Peace that are Reasonable, and Honourable, and Just, and upon which the War is founded, but in his pretended Treaties, chicanes and falsifies, and is altogether Insincere, then 'tis not the General's Fault if we can't have Peace; we are in for the War, and we must stand to it.

Indeed in the last dear Year of Corn, France was almost reduced to their last Shifts; their Sufferings could be call'd little less than a Famine, and most of the Powers of Europe did really believe that they must have sued for a Peace, if they had not been assisted; but whilst the Circumstances of this Peace were in Agitation, then did the good People of Great Britain and Ireland, the north part of them to Burgundy, and Champaign, by way of Holland, thro' the Maes; and the South Part of them from Dunkirk and Calais over-against Kent, beyond the Mouth of the Garroon on the Western Ocean, supply that Country with vast quantities of Corn, almost to the starving of their own People. Not one of them cried out for Peace, or blam'd the General, their Pockets being well fill'd; But swore in the Markets, over plentiful Nappy, that in a short time they would pull old Lewis out of his Throne.

As for our Generals avoiding Fighting, 'tis easie to guess out of what Quiver this Arrow of Scandal was drawn; for without doubt 'twas forg'd in his own Army; and seeing the Roman History is now much in Fashion, I shall give an Example, as an Answer to this Scandal, and without doubt 'tis home to the Purpose. Haniball had beaten the Romans in three great Battles of Ticinum, Trebia, and Thrasymene: 'Twas his Business to Fight the Romans wherever he could come at them; his Army being compounded of rough old Mercenary Soldiers of divers Nations, who are ready to Mutiny and Desert upon all Occasions, if they have not present Pay or continual Plunder; in this Extremity the old Fabius was chosen Dictator, or supream Commander; he was a good Man of War, and understood his Business; and for his Lieutenant, or Master of the Horse, which among them was all one, he chose one Minutius, the worst thing that ever he did; because in a short time he found him to be an Ungrateful, Conceited, Hot-headed Accuser. Fabius with great skill and caution avoided Battle by Coasting Hanibal on the sides of Hills in rough Ground, by Woods and Rivers, and hard Passes; because much inferior in Horse to the Carthaginian; and thereby gain'd time to confirm the Hearts of his Soldiers, and so make them capable by degrees to look the Enemy in the Face. Hanibal soon found that by no means he could draw in this wary old Gamester, but declar'd, that he fear'd nothing more than that Clowd which hung about the Hill Tops, least some time or other it should fall down and severely wet him. Winter coming on, and the Dictator being obliged to return home about some other Affairs; He left his Army to the Care of this Master of the Horse, with a strict charge to shun Fighting with all possible Care, and to follow the Example which he had set before him: He was prowd of this Opportunity of Commanding the Army, and believ'd himself the best and the ablest Man for it; he procured to have his Courage magnified at home among the common People, and that if he had a Command equal to the Captain General, he would soon give a better Account of Hanibal and his Army; that Fabius was afraid to look towards his Enemy, and thereby disheartned the Soldiers, who were otherwise naturally Brave; and by his Fearfulness suffered these Barbarians to Ravage in their Country, to their Ruine and Destruction. The Tribunes of the People, not much better than Captains of the Mob, were his particular Friends, and they complaining to the Senate, every where gave it out, that after this manner of Fabius his going on, the War would never have an end, that the City would be undone by perpetual Taxes; that all Trade was ceas'd, and nothing to be seen among the Commons, but a sad Prospect of growing Poverty.

The Senate was wearied out by these Factious Importunities, till at last 'twas granted, that the Master of the Horse should have equal Command with that Great Man who would preserve them from Ruine. Accordingly he receiv'd half of the Army to be under his Charge, by a Lot, for Fabius would not endure, because he foresaw what would come to pass, that it shou'd be in his Power, for one Day, to command the whole. Minutius, forsooth, to show his Bravery, march'd nearer to the Enemy. Hannibal had laid a Train for the Hotspur, and soon caught him; and both he and his Army had been soon cut to pieces if the Old General, not permitting private Revenge to interfere with the good of his Country, had not drawn down in very good Order, repuls'd the Ambush, and secur'd his Retreat. The best thing that Minutius cou'd do, was to beg Pardon for his Fault, and promise more regard to his Superiors for the future. So that you see 'tis the Experienc'd, Skilful, Old General who is best Judge of times of Fighting; and that Man who asperses his Honour is to be suspected as either wanting Judgment, or an Enemy to the Publick.

Another Scandal was lately rais'd against his Grace, as touching his good Conduct and Skill, as he is a General; and this is much among those sort of People, whose Mouths go off smartly with a Whiff of Tobacco, and fight Battles, and take Towns over a Dish of Coffee. They give out, like Men of great Understanding in the Art Military, that the Duke is more beholding to his Good-Fortune than his Skill, in the Advantages he has gain'd over the French, and that he may thank the Prince of Savoy, and the good Forces which he Commands, more than his own Skill in War, for his great Reputation.

The Good-Fortune of His Grace ought to be attributed to the good Providence of GOD, for which, both he and the whole Nation ought to be thankful. 'Tis a great Happiness to have such a Fortunate General; and, without doubt, the French King would purchase such another at any rate, if he could.

But then, Nullum numen abest, si sit Prudentia. The General that is Prudent, and Vigilant, and Temperate, Alert, and Industrious, with an humble Submission to the Will of the Almighty, takes the right way of obliging Fortune to be of his Side: Or, to speak better, the Blessings of Heaven to crown his Endeavours: For in War 'tis seldom known, (quite contrary to the Old Proverb) that in conducting Armies and fighting Battles, Fools have Fortune.

As for his Acting in Concert with the Heroick Prince of Savoy, who is, without doubt, one of the ablest Generals of the Universe, and chusing of him to be his Friend and Colleague, is one of the strongest Arguments of his Art and Knowledge: Mutual Danger, and mutual Principles of Honour, have entirely united them. In all difficult Points they presently agree, as if what one was Speaking, the other was Thinking of the same Matter at the very same time: And no Person can believe, that Prince Eugene would endure that any Person in the World should share with him in his Fame and Glory, unless such an Hero, whom he thinks in all Points to be his Equal. As for the Troops under his Command, 'tis evident to the World, that they excel all others; for the sake of their Countries they are prodigal of their Blood; and under such a General, by their own Confession, when they go to Action, think of nothing else but Victory and Triumph.

But Matters of Fact are the best Arguments. Amongst the great number which might be produc'd, I shall only Instance these two following; and I am sorry that those People who have not seen Marching or Embatteling Armies cannot be competent Judges of them. Let the first be in the first Campaign, in the first Year of Her Majesty's Reign. We were encamp'd on the Confines of Brabant, not far from a little Town call'd Peer; the Country round about is almost all great Heaths and large Commons; we were in full March betimes in the Morning, and, by the countenance of our March, 'twas suppos'd we should have a long and a late Fatigue; when, on a sudden, about Eleven a Clock, we had Orders to halt, and to encamp at the bottom of an Heath, behind some rising Grounds and great Sand-Hills, near a Place called Hilteren; and according to the Time that my Lord Duke had projected, Mareschal Boufflers, with his Army, was blunder'd upon us, within Shot of our Cannon, not knowing where we were. At that time we were superior to the French, especially in Horse; they could by no means avoid a Battle, the Mareschal was caught: And if the Deputies of the States, and their Generals, could have been perswaded to venture a Battle, in conjunction with the other Allies; and they were entreated enough, almost with Tears, by all the other Princes and Generals of the Army, 'tis very probable the French, under that great surprize, had been severely beaten. At last they stole away from us in a dark Night, and were glad of the Escape. And thus then you see the great Skill of our General, to entrap the French Mareschal in his March, in the middle of the Day, and to make him, in a manner, fall into his Arms.

The second Instance is from the Battle of Ramelies. A Stratagem well laid argues the great Dexterity and Penetration of a General; in deep hollow Ways, in close Bottoms, and nigh sides of Woods, Ambuscades are often laid, and, perhaps, as often discovered; but to bring an Ambush upon an Enemy, into the open Country, in the face of the Sun, requires an assured Skill, as well as a daring Courage. Thus 'tis said of the Great Hannibal, at the Battle of Cannæ, that in the open Field he brought an Ambush on the Backs of the Romans, which very much help'd to encrease their Terror and Confusion. And thus did our General, at the foremention'd Battle, but with a better Contrivance.

The French King had Intelligence given him, that all the Forces of our Army were not join'd, and accordingly sent positive Orders to his General, not to let slip that Opportunity of chastising the Insolence of the Allies, for that was the Expression; and indeed 'twas true, the Allies had been pretty bold with him several times before: and the Mareschal doubted not but to have time enough to execute his Master's Commands, before a good Body of Horse, which he understood to be at a great distance, could be able to come up and assist us. The Duke gave a pretty good Guess at the Monsieur's Designs, and before-hand had sent strict Order, that they, without the least delay, should speed immediately towards him, and in the middle of the Night, to halt at a Village where he had appointed, not above two Leagues from his Camp; and after a little Refreshment, and Preparation for Service, must be ready to move at break of Day, upon the first bruit of Cannon: For their resting in that Place, and at such a distance, would be much more to his Advantage than if they had join'd him.

The Business being thus order'd, he was resolv'd the Enemy should not take all the Pains in coming towards him, but to meet them on part of the Way. The French Right Wing, in which were their best

Troops, oppos'd our Left, and in their vigorous Charge had the better of the Allies: The Duke, with the other Generals, rallied them again; but finding it difficult to sustain the strong Impression of the Enemy, presently gave out, and it took among all the Squadrons in a Moment, That a great number of the best Troops in the World, who were their Friends, were just at their Heels with Sword in hand, ready to sustain them, that no Power of the Enemy could look them in the Face; which being seen to be true, as well as felt by the Enemy, they were soon repulsed, discourag'd, and put into Confusion, which was the first cause of the general Rout of their Army.

And thus then you see, that our General wants neither Conduct or Courage: And as 'twas once said to that Renown'd Captain Epaminondas, who having no Children, and being about to die of his honourable Wounds, that his two Battels of Leuctra and Mantinæa should be as two fair Daughters to preserve his Memory. So may we say, that the many Battles and Sieges, fought and won by our Great Marlborough, in the Provinces of Gelders, of Limbourg, of Brabant, of Flanders, of Artois, of Hainault, shall be far excelling the most numerous Progeny to eternize his Name.

The other false Reports that are spread among the People, by the Enemies of the Duke, are these; That his way of Living in the Army is Mean and Parsimonious, unbecoming the Honour and Dignity of his Post. That the Income and Revenue from the Profits of his Places are too much for a Subject: And that he minds nothing so much as getting of Riches. All which Reports are false and malicious, and only the Designs of his secret Enemies.

Wo be to them that call Evil Good, and Good Evil. Some of this was part of the False Accusation that was urged against Scipio the Asiatic, by the Malice and ill Nature of Cato and his Accomplices; That he had squandred away the Money of the Government, in a great measure, by his excessive Way of Living; for so his Magnificence was termed by them: That his vast Treats and luxurious Tables had some popular Design. And, to be sure, if our General should offer to live after any such manner, the Nation would be fill'd with perpetual Clamour, that he treated the Officers to make them his Creatures, and in a short time would set up for himself; for, without doubt, those things which other Men might do, tho' much inferior to the Duke, with a general Applause, in him would be Criminal, and of bad Consequence.

In all ancient Histories nothing is more highly prais'd in Princes and great Captains, than Temperance and Moderation in Meat and Drink. The Commander of the Army ought to be vigilant, that (as a good Prince once said) the People committed to his Charge may sleep more safely; and 'tis not to be conceiv'd how such a Person, who is loaded continually with foggy Intemperance, can be Careful, Active, Watchful, Alert, Thoughtful, Foreseeing, being all Qualities necessary for so great a Charge.

His Grace governs his Family abroad like a wise Master, with good Order and Method; every thing about him shines with a temperate Use, and a daily chearful Plenty, not only for his own Domesticks, but for many others; but then all this is in due time and season: He has no Constitution for an Intemperate Life, and the Loads of it would soon destroy him.

As for his great Profits in the Army, let us take a view of them: There is an Author call'd, The Examiner, who has been very diligent in searching into His Grace's Revenue: But I am sure, in his Perquisites belonging to the Army he can be no Judge; the Pay of a Captain General, by the Day, may be known to any one, I suppose 'tis set down in the Present State of England, as well as Master of the Ordnance, and Colonel of a Regiment of Foot-Guards; these are all his Military Employments, and the Pay of them as much his due, as the Pay of Three Shillings and Six-Pence is to an Ensign. The Earl of Rumney had all these Places except Captain-General; he was both a Lieutenant-General and an Ambassador, and enjoy'd them a long time, and yet I never heard of any Man that envied him, or found fault that he had too many Places. And 'tis a common thing for a great Mareschal of France to have many more Posts, and of much greater Profits.

Any young Clerk, who belongs to an Agent, can presently show how many Regiments of Horse, Foot, and Dragoons are in the Pay of Her Majesty, under the Duke; and everyone there, from a General to a Drummer, what their proper Pay is, nor can they be deceived. The Hospitals and the Artillery are paid accordingly, in an exact Method. The Pay of each particular Body is issued out to the Pay-masters of the Army, from the Pay-Master-General; and the Duke touches not a Farthing but what properly belongs to him. And whereas abundance of People complain, that almost all the Money of the Nation was, by the late Lord Treasurer, sent into Flanders to pay the Troops there; no matter what became of the other parts of the War. This I know to be true, That the mercenary or hired Forces, which are in our Pay, and are the greatest part of our Army under the Duke, being most of them Danes, Swiss, Saxons, and Palatines, all of the German kind, will not march one Foot, notwithstanding all the Perswasions that any General can use; no, not to save any King or Prince in the World, unless they are duly paid, at the appointed times, according to their first Agreement: but then, as soon as you shew the Gheldt, they presently Shoulder, and Stalk wheresoever you please.

What the Queen is pleas'd to allow the Duke for his Secret Service, because his Eyes and Ears must be in all Secret Cabinets, (and, without doubt, his Intelligence must be very good) it is not fit for me or the Examiner to know; or, for ought I can judge, any one else besides in the World.

The Perquisites of Safeguards and Contributions, which in all Times have belong'd to Generals, can't easily be valued, they are according to the Countries in which the War is carried. But for all these Profits to be ascrib'd to the Duke, (as in several Pamphlets 'tis evident they are) is very unreasonable; because there are two other Chief Generals besides, the Prince of Savoy for the Imperialists, and Count Tilly for the States, each of which will claim their Parts as well as His Grace; besides the gross of them, which are given to the States themselves: and yet we hear of no Complaint, or Papers printed against them, or in the least envied by any of the Nations under whom they serve.

In short, 'tis all the Reason that a conquering General, who fights our Battels, and must look the Powers of Europe in the Face, as he is distinguish'd by Titles of Honour, so where-ever he goes he ought to be attended with Plenty and Riches.

A Sea-Captain, after the Service of Nine or Ten Years, is usually Master of a very great Fortune, he Sails in his Coach with rich Liveries for his Colours, and Steers from his City to his Country-House unenvied, and without unmerciful Remarks. The honest Gentlemen in Town, call'd Agents, most of whom are risen from a mean Condition to be Members of Parliament, Justices of the Peace, and to purchase Estates, where-ever they can find out Land to be dispos'd of, who never ventur'd their Lives farther than from the Pay-Office to the Tavern; and yet they make a Figure in the World with a very good Grace, untouch'd, or not mark'd by any Observator.

But this has been the Fortune of the most glorious Persons, to be envied and persecuted whilst they are alive, and when taken away from us by some unlucky Accident, are desir'd too late, and lamented with a Witness.

If we observe, through the whole Nation, either here in this Capital, or in any other Parts of England, allowing but for proportion of Merit and Dignity, we shall find more People belonging to Offices of Docks and Yards, to Offices of Stores and Victualling, who have made as good use of the Places in which they serve, and with no greater Fatigue and Danger than Figuring and Writing, as the best and richest General in Europe.

When my Lord Marlborough had escap'd the Wars, and was return'd to the quiet of the Country, no Word was heard of him in Court or Town, no one talked of his Money, or Riches, or Estate; but no sooner was he again call'd to the High Station in which he now Acts, but Envy had presently found him out, even in the midst of Guards and Arms, and ever since has follow'd him close with all sorts of False-Reports, to this very time; as if nothing but his most excellent Qualities, and growing Glory, could make him Unfortunate.

Indeed Generals, tho' the most accomplish'd Heroes, are but Men, they are not Infallible, but may be mistaken as well as other Mortals, they are subject to Faults and Infirmities as well as their Fellow-Creatures; but then their great Services for the good of their Country ought to be cast into the Ballance, against their humane Mistakes; and not only Charity, but Self-consideration should give them very good Quarter, unless their Faults are prov'd to be Wilful and Contumacious.

I know not how it might happen to the Duke if he should chance to Miscarry, or be beaten in a Battle; God be prais'd, as yet he has never been foil'd: but then we must not suppose that he is Invincible, that Fortune will always be confin'd to the Pomel of his Sword. But this is certain, that the French King has not been severe to any of his Great Captains, tho', in their turns, they have been all beaten by the Prince of Savoy and the Duke, the Prince taking one of his chief Mareschals a Prisoner with him out of the midst of his Garison; the Duke another of them on the Banks of the Danube, with the greatest part of the Banners and Trophies of his almost captiv'd Army: there are no Outcries of the Common People for a Sacrifice to the Publick, nor base Reflections made on their Courage or Conduct; because 'tis suppos'd in all those fiery Ordeals of Battles, a General exerts all the Faculties and Powers of Body and Soul; he puts Nature on the stretch. And as my Lord Duke, at the conclusion of the great Battle of Blenheim said, I think to his Honour, that he believed he had pray'd more that Day than all the Chaplains of his Army.

Therefore let not People think, that those Gentlemen who are call'd to fight Battles make use of those Employments, in the heat of a bloody War, for Diversion or Pleasure. They who have been Spectators of what they do and what they suffer, will soon be perswaded, that no People under Heaven purchase their Profits and Honours at a dearer rate.

'Tis a great happiness to a Nation to have a generous Race of Warlike People, who, at all times, are ready to venture their Lives in the defence of it. Cowardice is the highest Scandal to a Country, and exposes it to be a Prey to every Invader, as well as a Scorn to their Neighbours. In all Histories of the World, they who dare die for the sake of their Country, have been esteem'd as a sort of Martyrs: And the People who are protected at Home in their Estates, Ease, Safety, and Liberties, ought not to grudge them of any of their Perquisites; but to bless God for such a gallant number of Martial Brethren, who drive the War at a great distance, so that we see none, we do but hear of it; for 'tis a sad thing to behold the Ravages, the Ruine, the Spoils, the Devastations of those Countries which happen to be the Seats of War.

When the Officers, coming from Flanders, after the Campaign, appear in the newest Fashions, which they bring over with them, with a good Ayre and genteel Mien, which is almost common to them, the People, who never saw the Hardships which they undergo, think them only design'd for Pleasure and Ease, and their Profession to be desir'd above any thing in the World besides. They often hear of Fights and Sieges, and of a great many Men kill'd in a few Hours; but because they see not the Actions, the Talk leaves but a small and transient Impression, and so in a small time is wip'd off and forgotten. But if they did but see them in a Rainy Season, when the whole Country about them is trod into a Chaos, and in such intolerable Marches, Men and Horses dying and dead together, and the best of them glad of a bundle of Straw to lay down their wet and weary Limbs: If they did but see a Siege, besides the daily danger and expectation of Death, which is common to all, from the General to the Centinel; the Watches, the Labours, the Cares which attend the greatest; the ugly Sights, the Stinks of Mortality, the Grass all wither'd and black with the Smoke of Powder, the horrid Noises all Night and all Day, and Spoil and Destruction on every side; I am sure they would be perswaded, that a State of War, to those who are engag'd in it, must needs, be a state of Labour and Misery; and that a great General, I mean such a one as the Duke of Marlborough, weak in his Constitution, and well stricken in Years, would not undergo those eating Cares, which must be continually at his Heart; the Toils and Hardships which he must endure, and the often Sorrows which must prick his Heart for ugly Accidents, if he has the least Spark of humane Commiseration, I say, he would not engage himself in such a Life, if not for the sake of his Queen and Country, and his Honour.

I come now to add a word or two of the government of the Forces under his Care. His own Example gives a particular Life to his Orders; and as no indecent Expression, unbecoming, unclean, or unhandsome Language ever drops from his Lips, so he is imitated by the genteel part of his Army: His Camps are like a quiet and well-govern'd City; and, I am apt to believe, much more Mannerly; Cursing and Swearing, and boisterous Words being never heard among those who are accounted good Officers: And, without doubt, his Army is the best Academy in the World to teach a young Gentlemen Wit and Breeding; a Sot and a Drunkard being scorn'd among them.

These poor Wretches, that are (too many of them) the refuse and off-scowrings of the worst parts of our Nation, after two Campaigns, by the Care of their Officers, and good Order and Discipline, are made Tractable, and Civil, and Orderly, and Sensible, and Clean, and have an Ayre and a Spirit that is beyond vulgar People.

The Service of GOD, according to the Order of our Church, is strictly enjoin'd by the Dukes special Care; and in all fixed Camps, every Day, Morning and Evening, there are Prayers; and on Sundays Sermons are duly perform'd with all Decency and Respect, as well as in Garisons. And, to be sure, the Good-Nature, and Compassion, and Charity of Officers express'd to the poor sick and wounded Soldiers, and to their Families in Garison, is more Liberal, and Generous, and Free, than usually we meet with in our own Country.

And now then I hope my good Country-men will not suffer themselves any longer to be impos'd on by false Reports, which are cunningly spread abroad among them, against a Gentleman, a Patriot, who ventures his Life, every Day, for their Safety, and is endeavouring to the utmost of his Power, under his Most Gracious Sovereign, by his Courage, his Skill, and his Wisdom, to bring the Common Enemy to Reason, and to procure them and our Allies, an honourable and lasting Peace.

'Tis a thing of ill Consequence to bring a Disreputation on the good Name of a General; and to lessen his Honour is to dispirit his Army: for when the Forces under his Command have once a mean Opinion of the Integrity, and Honour, and Conduct of their General, they may be drawn out and forced to Battle, but never be perswaded to think of Laurels and Victory.

'Tis an old Piece of Policy for an Enemy, if possible, to bring an Odium on the Honour of a General against whom he is to act. Thus did Hannibal, who, in his moroding Marches, had spared some Grounds belonging to the Dictator Fabius, not out of any respect or kindness to his Person, but to bring him into Envy and Suspicion among the People at Rome; and so 'twas given out by one of the Tribunes, that Hannibal and he had, as it were, made a Truce; that the drift of Fabius could be nothing else but to prolong the War, that he might be long in Office, and have the sole Government both of City and Armies. And, without doubt, the French King would have been very well satisfied, if this same Aspersion, which was lately spread abroad concerning our General, had taken the effect of having him laid aside, and put out of his Places. A Finish'd Hero does not grow up every Day, they are scarce Plants, and do not thrive in every Soil; He may be easily lost, but then that Loss cannot easily be repair'd; therefore there is great Reason to Value and Esteem him.

To conclude, As our great Commander is known to the World, or at least to the greatest part of it, to be Temperate, Sober, Careful, Couragious, Politick, Skilful, so he is Courteous, Mild, Affable, Humble, and Condescending to People of the meanest Condition. And as 'tis said of Moses, the Great, the Valiant Captain-General of Almighty God, for an immortal Title of Honour, that he was one of the Meekest Men upon the Earth; so, without doubt, our Captain-General, John Duke of Marlborough, has a great share of it.

A SEASONABLE WARNING AND CAUTION AGAINST THE INSINUATIONS OF PAPISTS AND JACOBITES IN FAVOUR OF THE PRETENDER

Being a Letter from an Englishman at the Court of Hanover.

And thou shalt teach these Words diligently unto thy Children, and shalt talk of them when thou sittest in thy House, and when thou walkest by the Way. Deut. vi. 7.

And what thou seest write in a Book. Rev. i. 11.

Why how now, England! what ailest thee now? What evil spirit now possesseth thee! O thou nation famous for espousing religion, and defending liberty; eminent in all ages for pulling down tyrants,[1] and adhering steadily to the fundamentals of thy own constitution:[2] that has not only secured thy own rights, and handed them down unimpaired to every succeeding age, but has been the sanctuary of other oppressed nations;[3] the strong protector of injured subjects against the lawless invasion of oppressing tyrants.

To thee the oppressed protestants of France owed, for some ages ago, the comfort of being powerfully supported, while their own king,[4] wheedled by the lustre of a crown, became apostate, and laid the foundation of their ruin among themselves; in thee their posterity[5] find a refuge, and flourish in thy wealth and trade, when religion and liberty find no more place in their own country.

To thee the distressed Belgii[6] owe the powerful assistance by which they took up arms in defence of liberty and religion, against Spanish cruelty, the perfidious tyranny of their kings, and the rage of the bloody Duke d'Alva.

From thee the confederate Hollanders[7] received encouragement to join in that indissoluble union which has since reduced the invincible power of the Spaniards, and from whence has been raised the most flourishing commonwealth in the world.

By thy assistance they are become the bulwark of the protestant religion, and of the liberties of Europe; and have many times since gratefully employed that force in thy behalf; and, by their help, thou, who first gavest them liberty, hast more than once rescued and preserved thy own.

To thee the present protestant nations[8] of Europe owe their being at this day freed from the just apprehensions of the growing greatness of France; and to thy power, when acting by the glorious protector of thy liberty, King William, is the whole Christian world indebted for depriving the French tyrant of the hopes and prospect of universal monarchy.

To thy blood, thy treasure, the conduct of thy generals, and the vigour of thy councils, are due, the glory, the fame, the praises, and the advantages of twenty years' war, for the establishing and restoring the liberty and religion of Europe.

When posterity shall inquire into the particulars of this long and bloody war; the battles, sieges, and stupendous marches of armies, which, as well with loss as with victory, have been the subject of thy history; it will for ever be frequent in their mouths; HERE the British troops, fighting with dreadful fury, and their usual constancy, shed their blood in defence of the protestant cause, and left a bloody victory to God's enemies and their own; as at Steenkirk, Landen, Camaret, Almanza, Brihenga, and the like: or, HERE the British troops, with their usual valour, carried all before them, and conquered in behalf of the protestant interest, and Europe's liberties; as at Blenheim, Ramilies, Barcelona, Oudenard, Sarragossa, Blaregnies, &c. Here the British navies triumphed over French greatness; as at Cherburgh, La Hogue, Gibraltar, &c. There their land forces reduced the most impregnable fortresses; as at Namur, Lisle, Menin, Tournay, &c.

And wherefore has all this English and British blood been spilt? Wherefore thy nation exhausted; thy trade sunk and interrupted; thy veins opened? Why hast thou struggled thus long, and with so much vigour, as well with French tyranny abroad, as popish factions at home, but to preserve entire the religion and liberties of Europe, and particularly of this nation, and to preserve our posterity from slavery and idolatry? Principles truly noble, worthy a nation's blood to protect, and worthy a nation's treasure to save.

But what has all this been for? And to what intent and purpose was all this zeal, if you will sink under the ruin of the very fabric ye have pulled down? If ye will give up the cause after ye have gained the advantage, and yield yourselves up after you have been delivered; to what purpose then has all this been done? Why all the money expended? Why all this blood spilt? To what end is France said to be reduced, and peace now concluded, if the same popery, the same tyranny, the same arbitrary methods of government shall be received among you again? Sure your posterity will stand amazed to consider how lavish this age has been of their money, and their blood, and to how little purpose; since no age since the creation of the world can show us a time when ever any nation spent so much blood and treasure to end just where they begun: as, if the hearts of our enemies prevail, we are like to do.

Let us reason a little together on these things, and let us inquire a little, why, and for what reason Britain, so lately the glory of Europe; so lately the terror of France, the bulwark of religion, and the destroyer of popery, should be brought to be the gazing-stock of the world? And why is it that her neighbours expect every hour to hear that she is going back to Egypt, and having given up her liberty, has made it her own choice to submit to the stripes of her taskmasters, and make bricks without straw.

We that are Englishmen, and live from home among the protestants of other nations, cannot but be sensible of this alteration, and we bear the reproaches of those who speak freely of the unhappy change which appears in the temper of our countrymen at home. It is astonishing to all the world to hear that the common people of England should be turned from the most rivetted aversions, to a coldness and indifference in matters of popery and the pretender: that they, who with so unanimous a resolution deposed the late King James, as well for his invasions of their liberty as of their religion; and who with such marks of contempt drove him and his pretended progeny out of the nation, should without any visible alteration of circumstances, be drawn in to favour the return of that race with all the certain additions of popish principles in religion; French principles in government; revenge for family injuries; restoration of abdicated and impoverished votaries; and the certain support of a party at home, whose fortunes and losses must be restored and repaired out of the ruins of their country's liberties.

To what purpose was the revolution? Why did you mock yourselves at so vast an expense? Why did you cry in your oppressions to God and the Prince of Orange to deliver you? Why did you rise as one man against King James and his popish adherents? Why was your fury so great, and your opposition so universal, that although he had a good army of veteran, disciplined troops, and a powerful assistance from France ready to fall in and join him, yet they durst not, when put all together, venture to look you in the face, but fled like darkness before the sun, like guilt before the sword of justice; or as a murderer from the avenger of blood? Was it all, that you might the better weaken yourselves by ages of war, and they might return again, and bind you like Samson, when your strength was departed?

When this was done, why did ye mock God with a thanksgiving,[9] and banter the world with your pretended praises to heaven for your deliverance? Why, when you appeared by your representatives in convention and in parliament, did you make so many fast days,[10] and days of prayer for the success of the arms you took up, and the war you carried on for the finishing and securing this great work, called the pulling down of popery? Was it all, that after having spent twenty years of war, and a sea of blood, ruined trade, exhausted your treasure, and entailed vast debts on your posterity; you should calmly open your doors to the fugitives you had found out, and let in again the popish tyranny you had driven away?

For what reason was it that you presented the crown to your benefactor, called him your deliverer, and made him your king; and having done so, maintained him upon the throne with so much vigour, fought under his banner in so many battles, and with so great animosity, and professed to stand by him against all his enemies at home and abroad? Why is he in so many addresses[11] styled the rescuer of this nation from popery and slavery? Why in so many acts of parliament[12] is he called the great deliverer of the nation? Why in so many sermons preached to men, and prayers put up to God, has he the title of "the instrument blessed by heaven to free these nations from popery and arbitrary government?" Was all this done, that your posterity being brought back into the bondage their fathers were delivered from, should with the same alacrity call him an invader, an usurper, a parricide, and their fathers, rebels and revolters?

Why was the crown entailed by so many provisoes, reserves, and limitations? Why the names of every person that should succeed, so expressly and particularly mentioned and set down?[13] Why so many acts of parliament[14] to secure that entail, and punish with death those who should reject or oppose it? Why was the settlement of the crown thought to be of so much consequence to the public good, that the two daughters of King James, the late blessed Queen Mary, and her present royal majesty, thought themselves bound to agree to the same for the safety and peace of their country, though it was in prejudice of the right and possession of their own father? Was it all, that the return of these things might be made upon the people with the greater weight, and that posterity might be prejudiced against the memory of the two royal sisters, as accessary to the ruin of their own father?

Why was King James and his popish posterity entirely excluded for ever from enjoying the imperial crown of these realms?[15] Why were so many acts of parliament made to extinguish the hopes of his race, and of their party, and for farther security of her majesty's person and government? Why was the settlement of the succession in a protestant line made the principal reason of uniting the two kingdoms together? And why was that union so vigorously opposed by all those that adhered to the jacobite interest? Was this to illustrate the return of the abdicated line, and by the greatness of the nation's endeavour for keeping out the pretender, to justify his using them accordingly when he comes in?

Why was the union declared to be unalterable, and, as some say, the power thereby taken out of the hands of the British parliament to change the settlement of the crown, or to name any other persons than those of the illustrious house of Hanover to succeed; and, above all, why was that severest of all oaths, the abjuration, contrived; by which it is rendered impossible for this nation, upon any pretence whatsoever, to receive the pretender but with the black stigma of an abominable perjury? Was this that, with the greater reverence to laws, and the greater regard to the solemnity of a national oath, we might all turn tail upon our principles, and in defiance of God and the laws, bow our knees to an abjured pretender?

For God's sake, Britons, what are you doing? And whither are you going? To what dreadful precipices are ye hurrying yourselves? What! are you selling yourselves for slaves to the French, who you have conquered; to popery, which you have reformed from; and to the pretender, whom you have forsworn? Is this acting like Britons; like protestants, like lovers of liberty? Nay, is it acting like men of reasonable souls, and men who have the light of common sense to act by?

That we may move you, then, to consider a little the grossness and absurdity of what you are doing, dear countrymen, be prevailed upon to debate a little with yourselves the state of your own case, which I shall briefly and plainly lay before you, thus:—

The government having thought fit, for reasons of state which I have no room to speak of in this place, to separate from the confederates, as well in the field as in treating with the French, and unhappily, I doubt, to make a separate peace; among the several improvements made of this by the enemies of Britain, this is one, viz., to encourage and increase the friends and interest of the pretender, and this they do upon several foundations. 1. Upon a supposition, or suggestion rather, that the ministry, because they have not thought fit to carry on the war, are therefore coming so entirely into the interest of France, that they must of necessity comply with the French king's demand of restoring the pretender. 2. Upon a like ill-grounded suggestion that the people of England and Scotland are more inclined to receive the pretender than they were formerly; in both which suppositions they grossly impose upon you, and yet by both they subtly carry on their crafty designs to delude the more ignorant part of the people of this nation, and to prepare them, as they think, for the coming of the pretender: as appears thus:—

1. By persuading the common people that the ministry are for the pretender, they, as far as in them lies, make a breach, a misunderstanding, and lay a foundation of jealousy and distrust between the people

and the government, enraging all those who are zealous for the Hanover succession, against the ministers of state, and so increasing the dangerous divisions that are among us, the closing and healing whereof is so much the duty and interest of all faithful subjects, that they may the more unanimously and sincerely join together against the pretender and all his adherents.

2. They intimidate those great numbers of people who, not so much acting by principle as example, are unwilling to show themselves in any cause which they have reason to fear is declining, and therefore act with the less zeal for the true interest, by how much they see, or think they see, the great ones of the nation fall off from it.

3. By suggesting that the common people of Great Britain are more inclined to the pretender than they were formerly, they think they bring them really to be so, and encourage all the endeavours of those who labour indefatigably all over the nation to have it so.

To undeceive the good people of Britain, therefore, in these things, dear countrymen, I beseech you to consider,

1. That whatever we may dislike of the proceedings of the ministry, and of the government, of which this is not the place to speak, there is no greater cheat can be put upon you than this is; for, whatever the jacobite party may promise themselves from the ministry, the ministry do not yet own their measures to tend that way; they do not act avowedly for the pretender; they do all things yet upon the supposition of the protestant succession, and carry it as in the interest of the house of Hanover; and to say they are for the pretender, is to charge them with the greatest treachery and hypocrisy, and is such an insolence in the jacobites, as the ministry ought to show their resentment at them for, and we hope they will do so; besides, there is a manifest difference between the fears of honest men, as that the measures of the ministry may encourage the friends of the pretenders and on the other hand, the insolent way of the jacobites claiming the ministry to be acting in their behalf; while therefore the ministry appear to act under the scheme of the Hanover succession, whether they are sincere or no, it is a good answer to a jacobite, whatever it is to another, to say, it is an unjustifiable assurance, and an affront to the government, to boast of the ministry being in the interest of the pretender.

It is also well worthy the consideration of the good people of Britain, that at the same time these men would have you believe that the ministers of state are bringing in the pretender, they would also have the ministers of state made believe, that the generality of the people are inclined to receive the pretender; by which double-faced fraud they endeavour to restrain you, the people of Britain, from appearing against the pretender, for fear of offending the government; and to restrain the said government in the same case, for fear of the people.

As they go on in these things with too much success, it is a very sad consideration to all true British protestants to find that a party of men among us, who yet call themselves protestants, fall in with them in many things, fomenting the divisions and breaches that are among us, weakening the constitution, and pursuing such principles as tend to destroy our liberties; by whose arts, and by the subtle management of which party, the revolution wears every day more and more out of date; the principles of liberty decay; the memory of King William sinks in our esteem; the heroic actions of that prince, which were once the just admiration of all the honest people of Great Britain, begin to be lost upon us, and forgotten among us, and to become as a mark of infamy to the nation!

Every considering protestant cannot but observe with horror, what swarms of popish priests from abroad, and jacobite emissaries at home, are spread about among us, and busily employed to carry on these wicked designs; how in disguise they run up and down the countries, mingling themselves in all companies, and in coffee-houses, and private conversation, endeavouring to insinuate with all possible subtlety, favourable notions of the pretender into the minds of the people, thereby to pave the way, and to prepare you for receiving him; such as, that he is the lawful son of King James; that he is a protestant in his heart; that he will abjure the errors of popery as soon as he has an opportunity; that the late King William promised to prove him a bastard, but never could do it; that it is hard to reject him for what was none of his own fault, and the like.

Although thinking men can and do see through these things, yet, as they are calculated and prepared to deceive the ignorant people in the country, it is earnestly desired of those who have their eyes open to the said popish delusions, that they would endeavour to undeceive their brethren and neighbours, and earnestly persuade them not to be imposed upon by the jesuitical insinuations of the popish faction, furnishing the poor honest people with just reasons for their adhering to the protestant settlement, and full answers to those who go about to deceive them: which answers are such as follow:—

1. It seems absolutely necessary to remind them of the reason of the late revolution; how King James II., by his popish counsellors, priests, and jesuits, had laid the foundation of overwhelming all our liberties, in an arbitrary, tyrannical government, ruling us without a parliament to redress our grievances, and, by a standing army, to execute forcibly his absolute commands; how he had engaged in the overthrow of our religion, by undermining the constitution of the Church of England, erecting an arbitrary ecclesiastical commission to dispossess our universities, and displace our ministers in every parish, and then to establish popery throughout the whole nation.

2. That in this distress, the whole nation applied themselves to the Prince of Orange, whose right to the succession made him justly appear as the proper person to assist and relieve this oppressed people; which prince came over at our invitation, was blessed with success, and all the favourers of popery and tyranny sunk at once; King James fled with his queen, and that person whom he called his son, and whom we now call justly the pretender.

3. Concerning the birth of this person, the nobility and gentry of England who invited over the prince, as may be seen by the memorial they presented to his highness, alleged, that there were violent presumptions that he was not born of the queen's body, which, however, they desired to leave to examination in a free parliament; which also the said prince expressed in his declaration, and that he was willing to leave the same to a free parliament.

4. That before a free parliament could be obtained, King James withdrew himself, and carried away his pretended son into the hands of the ancient enemies of this nation, and of our religion, the French, there to be educated in the principles of popery and enmity to this his native country.

By which action he not only declined to refer the legitimacy of his said son to the examination of the parliament, as the Prince of Orange had offered in his said declaration, but made such examination altogether useless and impracticable, he himself (King James) not owning it to be a legal parliament, and therefore not consenting to stand by such examination.

By the said abdication, and carrying away his said pretended son into the hands of the French to be educated in popery, &c., he gave the parliament of England and Scotland abundant reason for ever to exclude the said King James and his said pretended son from the government of these realms, or from the succession to the same, and made it absolutely necessary for them to do so, if they would secure the protestant religion to themselves and their posterity; and this without any regard to the doubt whether he was the lawful son of King James or no, since it is inconsistent with the constitution of this protestant nation to be governed by a popish prince.

So that there is now no more room to examine whether the said pretender be the lawful son of King James, or whether he is, or will turn to be a protestant, the examination of the legitimacy by parliament which was offered by the Prince of Orange in his declaration, having been declined by his father, and himself having been delivered up into the hands of the sworn enemies both of our religion, constitution, and nation.

If King James would have expected he should be received as his son, and succeed to his crowns, he should have suffered his birth to have been legally determined by the English and Scotch parliament at that time, and have left him in good protestant hands to have been educated in the protestant religion, and in the knowledge of the laws and constitutions of his country; in which case it was more than probable, had his birth appeared clear, and his hereditary right just, the parliament might have set the crown upon his head, and declared him king under the protection of their deliverer, the Prince of Orange: but to talk of it now, when his birth has never been examined or cleared up, and while he has been bred up to man's estate in popery, and that the worst sort, viz., French popery; and after the parliament of the respective kingdoms uniting in one, have by an unalterable, indissolvable union, settled and entailed the crown upon another head, viz., the present queen, and entailed it after her majesty in the most illustrious house of Hanover, the next of blood in a protestant line: to talk now of proving the birth of the pretender, and of his abjuring his errors and turning protestant, this is a fraud so absurd and ridiculous, that we hope the people of Great Britain can never be blinded with it.

Especially considering the party who talk of these things to us: and this ought to move the good people of Britain to receive the proposals of the pretender with indignation; for who are they, dear fellow-protestants! that persuade you to these things? Are they not the friends of France and Rome? Do not all the papists join with them? Do not all those who hated the revolution, and who long to restore arbitrary government, join with them?

Why, if he will abjure the Romish errors and turn protestant, why, I say, do the papists speak in his favour? Do any sect of religion love apostates! Those who forsake them and abjure them as heretical and erroneous! If they were not well assured that whatever appearing change he may make, he will still retain a secret affection to popery, they could not be rationally supposed to speak in his behalf.

But if that is not sufficient, what do they say to you as to his love of the liberty of his country? Has he been bred up in a tyrannical absolute court for nothing? Can he have any notion of government there but what is cruel, oppressive, absolute, and despotic? What principles of government will he come over with? and as he has sucked in tyranny with his milk, and knows no government but that of the most absolute monarch in the world, is this the man they would bring in to preserve the liberties and constitution of Britain?

When set upon the British throne, who are his allies and confederates? Will he be so ungrateful as not to be always at the devotion and command of the French king? a prince that took his father in a fugitive, an abdicated and ruined prince, when his fortunes were overthrown, and his crown taken from him; that made so many efforts to restore him, and hazarded his whole kingdom for it: if he forgets the kindness shown to his father, can he be so ungenerous, so unthankful, as to forget how the king of France nourished him from a child; how, after his father's death, he hazarded a second war to proclaim him king of Great Britain, and what expense he has been at to put him in possession of it? Should he forget all these obligations, he must be unfit to be called a Christian, much less a prince.

If he can act so barbarously to the French king, his benefactor, what must you Britons expect from him, who have done nothing to oblige him, but have for twenty-four years kept him and his father in exile, and treated them both with unsufferable indignity? If he can be ungrateful to the king of France, who has done so much for him, what must he be to you, who have done so much against him?

Again: if gratitude and honour have any influence upon him, if he has any sense of his obligation to the French king, will he not for ever be his most hearty, obedient, humble servant? Will he not always be in his interest, nay, ought he not to be so? Is he not tied by the laws of friendship and gratitude to be so?

Think, then, dear Britons! what a king this pretender must be; a papist by inclination; a tyrant by education; a Frenchman by honour and obligation: and how long will your liberties last you in this condition? And when your liberties are gone, how long will your religion remain? When your hands are tied; when armies bind you; when power oppresses you; when a tyrant disarms you; when a popish French tyrant reigns over you; by what means or methods can you pretend to maintain your protestant religion?

How shall the Church of England stand, when in subjection to the Church of Rome? You are now mixed with dissenters, and some are uneasy enough with them too; but our church will then be but a dissenting church; popery will be the establishment; the mass will succeed our common prayer, and fire and fagot instead of toleration, as you know was our case before; for it is not the first time the papists have been tried.

Nor did Queen Mary promise, nay, swear less than is now promised for the pretender; for she swore to the Gospellers of Suffolk to make no alteration in religion; and they, like the blinded protestants of this age, brought her in, for which they were the first that felt the fury and rage of the popish party, and so we have great cause to believe it would be again.

THE CONCLUSION

Consider, then, honest countrymen and protestants, what you are doing; look on your families; consider your innocent children, who you are going to give up to be bred in abominable superstition and idolatry; look on your dear country, which you are preparing to make the seat of war, blood, and confusion; look on your neighbours, who, while they are resisting this inundation, for you may be assured honest men will resist it to the last, you are to fight with, whose throats you must cut, and in whose blood you must dip your hands; and, lastly, consider yourselves; how free, how quiet, how in peace, plenty, and in protestant liberty you now live, but are with your own hands pulling down upon you, so far as you entertain thoughts of the pretender, the walls of your own security, viz., the constitution, and making way for your French popish enemies to enter; to whom your religion, your liberties, your estates, your families, and your posterity, shall be made a sacrifice, and this flourishing nation be entirely ruined.

In the last place, all that have any concern left for the good of their country, and for the preserving the protestant religion, will remember how much it is in the power of the people of Britain for ever to discourage all the attempts to be made in favour of these popish enemies, and to overthrow them in the execution; and it is on this foundation that this paper is made public. The late letter from Douay, written by some of that side, who very well understood the pretender's true interest, acknowledges this, and that if the people of England could not be wheedled and deluded into the design, it was never to be done by force.

And is this your case, Britons! Will you be ruined by a people whom you ought to despise? Have they not been twenty years trying your strength, till they find it impossible for them to master you? And are they brought to such a condition as to use all their arts and shifts to bring on a peace; and will you be brought now in cool thoughts, and after so long a struggle, to do that yourselves which you would never let them do; and which, without your most stupid negligence of yourselves, they could never do.

For this reason, I say, these lines are written, and this makes them just, and the argument rational. If I were to move you to what was not in your power, I should easily be answered, by being told, you could not do it; that you were not able, and the like; but is it not evident that the unanimous appearance of the people of Great Britain against the pretender would at once render all the party desperate, and make them look upon the design as utterly impracticable. As their only hope is in the breaches they are making in your resolutions, so if they should see they gain no ground there, they would despair, and give it over.

It would not be worth notice to inquire who are, and who are not for the pretender; the invidious search into the conduct of great men, ministers of state and government, would be labour lost: no ministry will ever be for the pretender, if they once may but be convinced that the people are steady; that he gets no ground in the country; that the aversions of the common people to his person and his government are not to be overcome: but if you, the good people of England, slacken your hands; if you give up the cause; if you abate your zeal for your own liberties, and for the protestant religion; if you fall in with popery and a French pretender; if you forget the revolution, and King William, what can you expect? who can stand by you then? Who can save them that will destroy themselves?

The work is before you; your deliverance, your safety is in your own hands, and therefore these things are now written: none can give you up; none can betray you but yourselves; none can bring in popery upon you but yourselves; and if you could see your own happiness, it is entirely in your power, by unanimous, steady adhering to your old principles, to secure your peace for ever. O Jerusalem! Jerusalem!

[1: Edward II., Richard II., Richard III., James II.]

[2: In the several barons' wars in the reign of King Stephen, King John, &c.]

[3: Especially of the persecuted protestants in the Low Countries, in Queen Elizabeth.]

[4: Henry IV., who turned papist, and with much difficulty granted liberty to his protestant subjects by the edict of Nantes.]

[5: The French refugees, who being received here, are grown rich and wealthy by our trade.]

[6: The Flemings, when threatened with the inquisition from Spain, under the reign of Philip II.]

[7: Under William Henry, the first Prince of Orange, who formed the revolt of the Dutch provinces, and laid the foundation of the States General and their commonwealth.]

[8: The circles of Swabia and Franconia, the Palatinate, and the countries of Hessia, Wirtemberg, and others.]

[9: The Thanksgiving for the Revolution.]

[10: Monthly fasts appointed the first Wednesday of every month during the war in King William's time.]

[11: Vid. The Collection of Addresses in King William's reign.]

[12: Act for Offering the Crown; The Claim of Right; Act for Security of his Majesty's Person and Government, &c.]

[13: Vid. The several Prayers ordered to be read in Churches upon the occasion of the Fasts in King William's time.]

[14: Vid. The Act of the Settlement, and the Act of the Union; the Act to extinguish the hopes of the Jacobites; and the Act for farther securing her Majesty's Person and Government.]

[15: Vid. The Act of Parliament for settling the Succession of the Crown on the illustrious House of Hanover.]

AN ANSWER TO A QUESTION THAT NOBODY THINKS OF, VIZ. BUT WHAT IF THE QUEEN SHOULD DIE

That we are to have a peace, or that the peace is made, what sort of peace, or how it has been brought about; these are questions the world begins to have done with, they have been so much, so often, and to so little purpose banded about, and tossed like a shuttlecock, from one party to another; the parties themselves begin to want breath to rail and throw scandal. Roper and Ridpath, like two Tom T—men, have thrown night-dirt at one another so long, and groped into so many Jakes's up to their elbows to find it, that they stink now in the nostrils of their own party. They are become perfectly nauseous to read; the nation is surfeited of them, and the people begin to be tired with ill-using one another. Would any tolerable face appear upon things, we might expect the people would be inclined to be easy; and were the eyes of some great men open, they may see this was the opportunity they never had before, to make the nation easy, and themselves safe. The main thing which agitates the minds of men now, is the protestant succession and the pretender. Much pains have been taken on both sides to amuse the world about this remaining dispute; one side to make us believe it is safe, and the other to convince us it is in danger. Neither side hath been able to expatiate upon the part they affirm. Those who say the protestant succession is secure, have not yet shown us any step taken, since these new transactions, for its particular security. Those who say it is in danger, have not so clearly determined, even among themselves, from what particular head of public management that danger chiefly proceeds. Both these uncertainties serve to perplex us, and to leave the thing more undetermined than consists with the public ease of the people's minds. To contribute something to that ease, and bring those whose place it is to consider of ways to make the people easy in this case, this work is made public. Possibly, the question propounded may not meet with a categorical answer. But this is certain, it shall show you more directly what is the chief question which the substance of things before us is like to turn upon; and to which all our questions seem to tend. Were the great difficulty of the succession brought to a narrow compass, though we might spend fewer words about it, we should sooner come to a direct answer. Before I come to the great and chief question upon which this affair so much seems to turn, it seems needful to put the previous question upon which so much debate has been among us, and let that be examined. This previous question is this: Is there any real danger of the protestant succession? Is there any danger that the pretender shall be brought in upon us? Is there any danger of popery and tyranny, by restoring the son, as they call him, of abdicated King James? This is the previous question, as we may now call it. It is well known that there are some people among us, who are so far from allowing that there is any such danger as the said question mentions, that they will have it to be a token of disaffection to the government to put the question, and are for loading whoever shall offer to start such a question, with characters and party-marks odious to good men, such as incendiary, promoter of discontents, raiser of faction, divider of the people, and the like: names which the writer of these sheets, at the same time, both contemns and abhors. He cannot see that he is any enemy to the queen, in inquiring as diligently as possible, whether there are any attempts to depose her, or dangerous prospects of bringing in the hated rival of her glory and dominion. It is so far from that, that it is apparently the duty of every true subject of her majesty, to inquire seriously, whether the public peace, the queen's safety, her throne, or her person, is in any danger from the wicked design of her, and her people's enemies. Wherefore, and for the joint concern every protestant Briton has in this thing, I shall make no difficulty, plainly and seriously to state, and to answer this previous question, viz., Whether there is any danger of the protestant succession from the present measures, and from the present people concerned? I am not ignorant of what has been said by some, to prove that the present ministry cannot be suspected of having any view to the pretender in any of their measures. The best reason which I have seen given upon that subject, is, that it is not their interest; and that as we have not found them fools that are blind to their own interest; that either do not understand, or pursue it. This we find handled sundry ways, by sundry authors, and very much insisted upon as a foundation for us to build upon. We shall give our thoughts upon it with plainness, and without fear or favour. Good manners require we should speak of the ministry with all due regard to their character and persons. This, a tract designed to inquire seriously of a weighty and essential, not a trifling thing, which requires but a trifling examination; nor shall it be handled here with satire and scurrility. We approve neither of the flatteries of one side, nor the insultings of the other. We shall readily and most willingly join with those who are of opinion that it is not the interest of the ministry to be for the pretender, and that the ministry are not blind to, or careless of, their own interest; and consequently, that the ministry cannot be for the pretender. This I hope may be called a direct answer. When I say "cannot," I must not be understood potentially, that they have no moral capacity; but they cannot without such inconsistencies, contradictions, and improbable things happening in, which render it highly irrational so much as to suppose it of them. To shut the door against any possibility of cavil, it may be needful also to take it with us as we go, what we mean by the words "be for" the pretender; and this can be no otherwise understood, than to have a design, however remote, and upon whatever views, to bring him in to possess the throne of these kingdoms. The matter then being laid down thus, as sincerely and plainly as possible, we come to the question point-blank, and think it our duty to say with the greatest sincerity, that we do not believe the ministry are in any kind, or with any prospect, near or remote, acting for or with a design or view to bring in the pretender. Having granted this, we must, however, to prevent any breaking in, by way of cavil on one hand, or triumph on the other, subjoin immediately, that we do not in the least grant by this that the protestant succession is in no danger, even from several of the measures now taken in the world. It is far from any reflection upon the ministry to say that, however they may act upon a right sincere principle for the protestant succession in all they do, which, as above, we profess to believe, yet that many of the tools they make use of are of another make, and have no edge to cut any other way; no thoughts to move them towards any other end; no other centre, which they can have any tendency to; that the pretender's interest is the magnet which draws them by its secret influence to point to him as their pole; that they have their aim at his establishment here, and own it to be their aim; and as they are not shy to profess it among themselves, so their conduct in many things makes it sufficiently public. This is not meant as any reflection upon the ministry for making use of such men: the late ministry did the same, and every ministry will, and must employ men sometimes, not as they always join with them in their politic principles, but as either the men are found useful in their several employments, or as the ministry may be under other circumstances, which makes it necessary to them to employ them. Nor, as the Review well enough observed, does it follow that because the ministry have employed or joined with jacobites in the public affairs, that therefore they must have done it with a jacobite principle. But let the ministry employ these men by what necessity, or upon what occasion they will, though it may not follow that the ministry are therefore for the pretender, yet it does not also follow that there is no danger of the protestant succession from the employing those sort of people: For, what if the queen should die?

The ministry, it is hoped, are established in the interest of their queen and country; and therefore it has been argued, that supposing the ministry had the pretender in their eye, yet that it is irrational to suggest that they can have any such view during the life of her present majesty. Nay, even those professed jacobites, who we spoke of just now, cannot be so ungrateful to think of deposing the queen, who has been so bountiful, so kind, so exceeding good to them, as in several cases to suffer them to be brought into the management of her own affairs, when by their character they might have been thought dangerous, even to her person; thus winning and engaging them by her bounty, and the confidence that has been placed in them, not to attempt anything to her prejudice, without the most monstrous ingratitude, without flying in the face of all that sense of honour and obligation, which it is possible for men of common sense to entertain. And it can hardly be thought that even papists themselves, under the highest possessions of their religious zeal, can conquer the native aversions they must have to such abominable ingratitude, or to think of bringing in the pretender upon this protestant nation, even while the queen shall be on the throne. But though this may, and some doubt that also, tie up their hands during the queen's life, yet they themselves give us but small reason to expect anything from them afterward, and it will be hard to find anybody to vouch for them then. These very jacobites, papists, and professed enemies to the revolution, may be supposed upon these pretensions to be quiet, and offer no violence to the present establishment while her majesty has the possession, and while that life lasts, to which they are so much indebted for her royal goodness and clemency. But what would they do if the queen should die?

Come we next to the French king. We are told, that not the French king only, but even the whole French nation, are wonderfully forward to acknowledge the obligation they are under to the justice and favour which they have received from her majesty, in the putting an end to the war; a war which lay heavy upon them, and threatened the very name of the French nation with ruin, and much more threatened the glory of the French court, and of their great monarch, with an entire overthrow, a total eclipse. A war which, by their own confession, it was impossible for them long to have supported the expenses of, and which, by the great superiority of the allies, became dreadful to them, and that every campaign more than the other; a war which they were in such pain to see the end of, that they tried all the powers and courts in Christendom, who were the least neutral, to engage a mediation in order to a treaty, and all in vain; and a war which, if her majesty had not inclined to put an end to, must have ended perhaps to the disadvantage and confusion of both France and Spain, if not of all Christendom. The obligations the French are under for the bringing this war to so just and honourable a conclusion are not at all concealed. Nay, the French themselves have not been backward to make them public. The declarations made by the French king of his sincerity in the overtures made for a general peace, the protestations of his being resolved to enter into an entire confidence, and a league offensive and defensive with the queen's majesty for the preservation of the peace of Christendom, his recognition of her majesty's just right to the crown, his entering into articles to preserve the union, acknowledging the ninth electorate in favour of the house of Hanover, and joining in the great affair of the protestant succession. As these all convince the world of the necessity his affairs were reduced to, and the great advantages accruing to him by a peace, so they seem to be so many arguments against our fears of the French entering into any engagements against the crown of Britain, much less any against the possession of the queen during her life. Not that the honour and sincerity of the king of France is a foundation fit for her majesty or her people to have any dependence upon; and the fraction of former treaties by that court, when the glory of that monarch, or his particular views of things has dictated such opportunity to him as he thought fit to close with, are due cautions to us all not to have any dependence of that kind. But the state of his affairs, and the condition the war has reduced him to, may give us some ground to think ourselves safe on that side. He knows what power he has taken off from his enemies in making peace with her majesty; he knows very well with what loss he sits down, how his affairs are weakened, and what need he has to take breath after so terrible a war; besides the flame such an action would kindle again in Europe; how it would animate this whole British nation against him, in such a manner, and endanger bringing in a new war, and perhaps a new confederacy upon him so violently, and that before he would be in a condition to match them, that no one can reasonably suppose the French king will run the hazard of it. And these things may tend to make some people easier than ordinary in the affair of the succession, believing that the French king stands in too much need of the favour of the queen of Great Britain, whose power it well behoves him to keep in friendship with him, and whose nation he will be very cautious of provoking a third time, as he has already done twice, to his fatal experience. All these things, we say, may seem pretty well to assure us that nothing is to be feared on that side so long as her majesty lives to sit upon the British throne. But all leaves our grand question unanswered; and though we may argue strongly for the French king's conduct while the present reign continues, yet few will say, What he will do if the queen should die?

Nay, we may even mention the pretender himself, if he has any about him whose councils are fit to be depended upon, and can direct him to make a wise and prudent judgment of his own affairs; if he acts by any scope of policy, and can take his measures with any foresight; most easy is it for them to see that it must be in vain for him to think of making any attempt in Britain during the life of the queen, or to expect to depose her majesty, and set himself up. The French power, upon which he has already in vain depended, as it has not hitherto been able to serve him, or his father, but that their exile has continued now above twenty-four years, so much less can he be able to assist him now, while he has been brought as it were to kneel to the British court to put an end for him to this cruel destructive war; the reason is just spoken to, viz., that this would be to rekindle that flame which he has gotten so lately quenched, and which cost him so much art, so much management, so much submission to the allies, to endeavour the quenching of before. To attack the queen of Great Britain now in behalf of the pretender, would not only be in the highest degree ungrateful, perfidious, and dishonourable, but would for ever make the British court, as well as the whole nation, his violent and implacable enemies; but would also involve him again in a new war with all Europe, who would very gladly fall in again with Britain to pull down more effectually the French power, which has so long been a terror to its neighbours; so that the pretender can expect no help from the king of France. As to what the pope, the Spaniard, and a few petty popish powers, who might pretend upon a religious prospect to assist him, and with whose aid, and the assistance of his party here, he may think fit to hazard an attempt here for the crown, it is evident, and his own friends will agree in it, that while the queen lives, it is nonsense, and ridiculous for them to attempt it; that it would immediately arm the whole nation against them, as one man; and in human probability it would, like as his supposed father was served at the revolution, be the ruin of his whole interest, and blow him at once quite out of the nation. I believe that there are very few who alarm themselves much with the fears of the pretender, from the apprehension of his own strength from abroad, or from his own party and friends at home here, were they once sure that he should receive no assistance from the king of France. If then the king of France cannot be reasonably supposed either to be inclined, or be in a condition to appear for him, or act in his behalf, during the life of the queen, neither can the pretender, say some, unless he is resolved to ruin all his friends, and at last to ruin himself, make any attempt of that kind during her majesty's life. But what if the queen should die?

Having then viewed the several points of the nation's compass whence our danger of jacobite plots and projects against the protestant succession may be expected to come, let us now inquire a little of the state of the nation, that we make a right estimate of our condition, and may know what to trust to in cases of difficulty, as they lie before us. In doing this, as well to avoid giving offence to the people now in power, as to the entering into the quarrels which engage the present contending parties in this divided nation, we shall allow, however some may think fit to question it, the main debate; and grant this for the present as a fundamental, viz., That we are in no danger of the pretender during this queen's reign, or during this ministry's administration under her majesty; and avoiding all contention of that kind, shall allow our condition to be safe in every article as we go along, for so long as the queen lives, referring the observation of things in every head to those who can answer the main question in our title, viz., But what if the queen should die?

First of all, it may be noticed, that the present safety of this nation, whether we respect liberty, religion, property, or public safety and prosperity, depends upon this one fundamental, viz., that alluding reverently to that text of Scripture, we are all built upon the foundation of the late revolution, established law and right being the chief corner-stone. By this it is that her majesty is made our queen, the entail of the crown being reserved in the remainder to her majesty in the act of settlement made at the filling up the vacant throne, and by all those subsequent acts which her majesty's title was confirmed by, during the life of the late king. This revolution is that upon which the liberties and religion of this nation were rebuilt after the conflagration that was made of them in the calamitous times of King Charles II., and King James II., and from hence to the love of liberty which is found almost to be naturally placed in the hearts of true Britons; and upon the view whereof they have acted all along in the late war, and in all their transactions at home has obtained the title of a "revolution principle." Noting this then, as above, that her majesty is our queen by virtue of the revolution, and that during her reign that establishment alone must be the foundation of all her administration, this must effectually secure us against any apprehension that the persons acting under her majesty can act in behalf of the pretender during her majesty's life; for that they must immediately overthrow the throne, turn the queen out of it, and renounce the revolution, upon which her majesty's possession is established: as the revolution, therefore, is the base upon which the throne of her majesty is established, so her majesty, and all that act under her, are obliged to act upon the foot of the said revolution, even will they, nil they, or else they sink immediately out of rightful power to act at all; her majesty's title would fall to the ground, their own commissions would from that hour be void; they must declare their royal mistress and benefactress a subject to the pretender, and all her pretences of rightful possession injurious, and an usurpation. These things being so plain, that he that runs may read them, seem to stop all our mouths from so much as any suggestion that anybody can attempt to bring in the pretender upon us during the life of her present majesty. But what if the queen should die?

Subsequent to the revolution, many essential things are formed by our parliaments and government for the public good, on the foundation of which much of the present peace of the nation is founded; and while the said revolution-foundation stands fast, there is good ground to believe those essential points shall be preserved. If then we are satisfied that the revolution principle shall subsist as long as the queen lives, then for so long we may have good ground to believe we shall enjoy all those advantages and benefits which we received from the said revolution. But still, when we look back upon those dear privileges, the obtaining of which has cost so much money, and the maintaining of which has cost so much blood, we must with a deep sigh reflect upon the precarious circumstances of the nation, whose best privileges hang uncertain upon the nice and tender thread of royal mortality, and say we are happy while these last, and these may last while her majesty shall live. But what if the queen should die?

Let us descend to some other particulars of those blessings which we do enjoy purely as the effect of the revolution, and examine in what posture we stand with respect to them, and what assurance we have of their continuance: and first, as to TOLERATION. This was the greatest and first blessing the nation felt after the immediate settlement of the crown, which was established by virtue of the revolution engagement, mentioned in the Prince of Orange's declaration. The design of this law, as it was to give liberty for the worship of God to such dissenters as could not conform to the Church of England, and to give ease to tender consciences, so as by the law itself is expressed; it was to ease the minds of their majesties' subjects, and to give general quiet to the nation, whose peace had been frequently disturbed by the violence of persecution. We have seen frequent assurances given of the inviolable preservation of this toleration by her majesty from the throne in her speeches to the parliament; and during her majesty's reign, we have great reason to hope the quiet of the poor people shall not be broken by either repealing that law, or invading the intent and meaning of it while in force; and there are a great many reasons to hope that the present ministry are so far convinced of the necessity of the said toleration, in order to preserve the peace, and the common neighbourhood of people, that they can have no thought of breaking in upon it, or any way making the people who enjoy it, uneasy. Nay, the rather we believe this, because the ferment such a breach would put the whole nation into is not the safest condition the government can be in upon any account; and as the ministry cannot be supposed to desire to give uneasiness and provocation to the commons, but rather to keep them easy and quiet, and prevent the enemies of the present management from having any handle to take hold of to foment distractions and disturbances among the people, it cannot be thought that they will push at the toleration, so as to deprive the people of so considerable a thing. But after the present happy establishment shall have received such a fatal blow as that will be of the queen's death, and when popish pretenders, and French influences, shall prevail, it may well be expected then, that not toleration of dissenters only, but even of the whole protestant religion, may be in danger to be lost; so that, however secure we are of the free enjoyment of liberty of religion during the queen's life, we may be very well allowed to ask this question with respect to, not toleration only, but the Church of England also, viz., what will become of them, If the queen should die?

From toleration in England, come we to the constitution of religious affairs in Scotland; and here we have different views from what the case in England affords us; the powerful interest of jacobitism, if it may be said to be formidable anywhere, is so there. The enemies of the revolution are all the implacable enemies of the church establishment there: nay, many thousands are the declared enemies of the revolution, and of the queen's being upon the throne, from a mere implacable aversion to the presbyterian kirk, which is erected and established by that very revolution which has set the queen upon the throne. The union, which has yet farther established that presbyterian kirk, is for that reason the aversion of the same people, as it is the aversion of the jacobites, by being a farther confirmation of the Hanover succession, and a farther fixing the queen upon the throne. Now, as it is sure, that as before, while the queen lives, and the revolution influence carries its usual force in the kingdoms now united, the presbyterian kirk must and will remain, and all the little encroachments which have been made upon the kirk, as it may be observed, though they have created uneasiness enough, yet they still seem to suppose that the establishment itself cannot be overthrown. The union and the revolution settlement remain in Scotland, and must remain, as is said; while the queen lives we can have no apprehensions of them; the reasons are given above; and as we said before, we are to take them for granted in this discourse, to avoid other cavils. While then the revolution and the union are to be the foundation of the administration in Scotland, the presbyterian established church government there must also remain as the only legal kirk constitution, and so long we can entertain no fears of anything on that account. But what if the queen should die?

From such religious concerns as effect presbyterians, and other sectaries, or dissenters, as we call them, let us take a look at the remote danger of the Church of England. We have had a great deal of distraction in the time of the late ministry about the danger of the church; and as it appears by the memorial of the church of England, published in those times, and reprinted since; by the sermons of Dr. Sacheverell, and the eminent speeches at his trial, that danger was more especially suggested to come from the increase of dissenters here, the ministry of the whigs, and the establishing presbyterianism in the north of Britain. These things being in a great measure now overthrown by the late change of the ministry, and the new methods taken in the management of the public affairs, the people, who were then supposed to aim at overthrowing the ministry of those whigs, are pleased to assure us of the safety and flourishing condition of the church now more than ever; while the other party, taking up the like cry of the danger of the church, tells us, that now a real visible appearance of danger to the church is before us; and that not only to the church of England as such, but even to the whole interest and safety of the protestant religion in Britain; that this danger is imminent and unavoidable, from the great growth and increase of popery, and professed jacobitism in the nation. This indeed they give but too great demonstrations of from the spreading of popish agents among us, whose professed employment it is to amuse and impose upon the poor country people, as well in matters of jacobitism as of religion, and the great successes these emissaries of Satan have obtained in several parts of Britain, but especially in the north. Now, though we cannot but acknowledge but that much of this alarm is justly grounded, and that the endeavours of popish and jacobite agents and emissaries in divers parts of Britain are too apparently successful, yet as wise men could never see into the reality of such danger, as was by some people pretended to be impending over the church in the time of the late ministry, so neither can we allow that popery is so evidently at the door at this time, as that we should be apprehensive of having the church of England immediately transversed, and the protestant religion in Britain: and one great reason for this opinion is, that her majesty, who is a zealous professor of the protestant religion, and has been bred up in the bosom of the church of England, is so rooted in principle, and has declared from her very infancy such horror and aversion to popery, that it cannot enter into any true protestant thoughts to apprehend anything of that kind, while her majesty lives. But, Lord have mercy upon us! What if the queen should die?

From religious matters, come we next to consider civil interest, liberties, privileges, properties; the great article that in the late revolution went always coupled in the nation's negative with that of religion, as if they were woven together, and was always cried upon by the mob in one breath, viz., No popery, no slavery. The first of these concerns our civil interest; such as the public credit, by the occasions of a long and expensive war, and to prevent levying severe taxes for the carrying on the war, such as would be grievous to trade, oppressive to the poor, and difficult to be paid. The parliament, for the ease of the subjects, thought fit, rather to lay funds of interest to raise money upon, by way of loan, establishing those interests, payable as annuities and annual payments, for the benefit of those who advanced their money for the public service. And to make these things current, that the public credit might be sacred, and the people be made free to advance their money, all possible assurances of parliament have been given, that the payments of interests and annuities shall be kept punctually, and exactly according to the acts of parliament, that no misapplications of the money shall be made, or converting the money received upon one to make good the deficiency of the other; and hitherto the injunctions of that kind have been exactly observed, and the payments punctually made, which we call the credit of the nation. At the first of the late change, when the new ministry began to act, the fright the people were put in upon the suggestion of some, that all the parliamentary funds should be wiped off with a sponge, was very considerable; and the credit of those funds sunk exceedingly with but the bare apprehension of such a blow, the sums being infinitely great, and the number of indigent families being incredibly many, whose whole substance lay in those securities, and whose bread depended upon those interests being punctually paid; but wiser men saw quickly there was no ground for those fears; that the new ministry stood upon a foot that could no more be supported without the public credit than those that went before them; that especially while they were under a necessity of borrowing farther sums, they behoved to secure the punctual paying of the old; and by making the people entirely easy, not only take from them the apprehensions they were under of losing what they lent already, but make them forward and willing to advance more to this purpose, they not only endeavoured to give the people all satisfaction that their money was safe, and that the funds laid by the parliament in the former ministry should be kept sacred, and the payments punctually made, but took care to obtain parliamentary securities, by real funds to be settled for the payment of those debts contracted by the former ministry, and for which no provision was made before. This was the establishment of a fund for payment of the interests of the navy debt, ordnance, victualling, transport, &c., to the value of seven or eight millions, which is the substance of what we new call the South-sea stock. By this means the public credit, which it was suggested would receive such a blow at the Change as that it should never recover again, and that it would be impossible for the new ministry to raise any needful sums of money for the carrying on the war, or for the public occasions, recovered itself so as that the government hath ever since found it easy to borrow whatever sums they thought fit to demand, in the same manner as before. Now that these loans are safe, no man that weighs the circumstances of the ministry and government, and the circumstances of the people, can doubt; the first being in a constant necessity of supporting the public credit for the carrying on the public affairs, on any sudden emergency that may happen, and being liable to the resentment of parliament, if any open infraction should be made upon the funds, which touches so nearly the honour of the parliaments, and the interest of most of the best families in the nation. While this is the case, we think it is not rational to believe that any ministry will venture to attack parliamentary credit, in such a manner; and this will eminently be the case as long as her majesty sits on the throne. Nor can a thing so barefacedly tyrannical and arbitrary, and, above all, dishonourable and unjust, be suggested as possible to be attempted in the reign of so just and conscientious a prince; so that we may be very willing to allow that there is not the least danger of the public faith being broken, the public credit lost, the public funds stopped, or the money being misapplied. No cheat, no sponge, while her majesty lives. But, alas for us! What if the queen should die?

From this piece of civil right, come we to those things we call liberties and privileges. These may indeed be joined in some respects; but as we are engaged in speaking particularly to such points, wherein our present dangers do or do not appear, it is proper to mention them apart. Privileges may be distinguished here from liberties, as they respect affairs of trade, corporations, parliaments, and legislature, &c. Liberty, as they respect laws, establishments, declared right, and such like. As to the first, from the revolution to this time, they have not only been confirmed, which we had before, but many privileges added to the people, some of which are essential to the well-being of the kingdom. All the quo warrantos against corporation privileges, the high commission court against the church's privileges extending prerogative in detriment of the subject's natural right, and many such things, which were fatal to the privileges of this protestant nation, were laid aside, and received their just condemnation in the revolution; and not so only, but the privileges obtained since the revolution by consent of parliament, are very considerable; such as the toleration to this part of Britain, and the establishment of the church of Scotland; for the north part; in matters of religion; such as the triennial election of parliaments; in civil affairs, such as the several corporations granted upon really useful foundations in trade; as the bank company, &c., and such like. These and many more, which may be named, and which these are named only as heads of, are secured to us by law; and those laws yet again made sure to us by the honour and veracity of her majesty, and as long as her majesty's life is spared to these nations, we have great reason to believe we shall rather increase than lose our privileges. But what if the queen should die?

Our LIBERTIES, which come next in order, may be summed up in what we call legal, and native right; or such as by the natural consequence of a free nation, and a just government; or such as by mutual assent and consent of sovereign and subject, are become the legal right of the latter. These, needless to be enumerated here, are summed up into one; or are expressly enacted by statute law, and thereby become fundamental to the constitution. These receive no wound, but one of these two ways, either by open infraction and contempt of right, or by dispensing arbitrary power; both of which, by the many assurances from the throne, by the constant jealousies of parliaments, and the full liberty they have more of late than ever taken to examine into, and censure breaches of the laws, we are very well assured shall not be attempted in her majesty's time: nay, on the contrary, the superiority, and influence of parliaments over and upon the management of public matters, nay, even their influence upon the royal majesty of the sovereign, has been such, and has in such a manner insensibly increased of late, that the like has never been known or practised in this nation for some ages before. We see her majesty declines extending her prerogative, either to the detriment of her subjects, in cases civil or religious, and wherein it might be so extended; nay, when even the parliament have desired her to extend it: so that we have a great satisfaction in the safety of our established liberties, and that no tyrannical, arbitrary invasions of right shall be made during her majesty's reign. But what if the queen should die?

In like manner for our properties, our estates, inheritance, lands, goods, lives, liberties, &c. These are effectually secured by laws of the land, and the sovereign in this country, having no right, but by law, to any part of the subject's estate, causes that estate to be called PROPERTY. The kings and queens of Britain are monarchs limited to act by the laws. When they cease to rule by law, the constitution is broken, and they become tyrants, and arbitrary, despotic invaders of right. This is declared by the revolution, wherein the rights of the subject are openly, not set down only, but claimed, demanded as what justice required should be granted to them, and as what the sovereign, as aforesaid, has no right, no pretence, no just authority to take, or detain from him. This is the great capital and fundamental article of Magna Charta, and the foundation upon which all the laws subsequent and consequential to Magna Charta have been made. [No freeman shall be taken or imprisoned, or be disseized of his freehold, or liberties, or free customs, or be outlawed, or exiled, or otherwise destroyed; nor we will not pass upon him, nor condemn him, but by lawful judgment of his peers, or by the law of the land. Magna Charta, cap. xxix.] The words are plain and direct; and as to the subject we are now upon, they require no comment, no explication. Whatever they do, as to pleading in law the proof of the subject's right to the free possession of his own property, is also the less needful to enlarge upon here, because it is acknowledged in full and express terms by the sovereign, as well in practice, as in expression. Her majesty, adhering strictly to this, as a rule, has from the beginning of her reign made it her golden rule, to govern according to law. Nor, while the establishment of the crown itself is built upon the legal constitution of this nation, can it be otherwise here: that prince that governs here and not by law, may be said rather to oppress than to govern; rather to overrule, than to rule over his people. Now it cannot without great and unjustifiable violence to her majesty's just government, be suggested, that we are in any danger of oppression during the righteous administration of her majesty's reign. The queen raises no money without act of parliament, keeps up no standing army in time of peace, disseizes no man of his property or estate; but every man sits in safety under his own vine, and his fig-tree; and we doubt not but we shall do as long as her majesty lives. But what if the queen should die?

Possibly cavils may rise in the mouths of those whose conduct this nice question may seem to affect, that this is a question unfit to be asked, and questionless such people will have much to say upon that subject; as that it is a factious question, a question needless to be answered, and impertinent therefore to be asked; that it is a question which respects things remote, and serves only to fill the heads of the people with fears and jealousies; that it is a question to which no direct answer can be given, and which suggests strange surmises, and amuses people about they know not what, and is of no use, but to make people uneasy without cause.

As there is no objection, which is material enough to make, but is material enough to answer, so this, although there is nothing of substance in it, may introduce something in its answer of substance enough to consider: it is therefore most necessary to convince the considering reader of the usefulness and necessity of putting this question; and then likewise the usefulness and necessity of putting this question NOW at this time; and if it appear to be both a needful question itself, and a seasonable question, as to time, the rest of the cavils against it will deserve the less regard. That it is a needful question, seems justified more abundantly from a very great example, to wit, the practice of the whole nation, in settling the succession of the crown. This I take to be nothing else but this: the queen having no issue of her body, and the pretender to the crown being expelled by law, included in his father's disastrous flight and abdication; when the parliament came to consider of the state of the nation, as to government as it now stands; that King William being lately dead, and her majesty with universal joy of her people, being received as queen, the safety, and the lasting happiness of the nation is so far secured. But what if the queen should die?

The introduction to all the acts of parliaments for settling the crown, implies thus much, and speaks directly this language, viz., to make the nation safe and easy in case the queen should die: nor are any of these acts of parliament impeached of faction, or impertinences; much less of needless blaming the people, and filling their heads with fears and jealousies. If this example of the parliament is not enough justifying to this inquiry, the well known truth, upon which that example of parliament is grounded, is sufficient to justify it, viz., we all know the queen must die. None say this with more concern and regret than those who are forwardest to put this question, as being of the opinion above said, that, we are effectually secured against the pretender, and against all the terrifying consequences of the Frenchified governors, during her majesty's life. But this is evident, the queen is mortal, though crowned with all that flattering courtiers can bring together, to make her appear great, glorious, famous, or what you please; yet the queen, yea, the queen herself, is mortal, and MUST die. It is true, kings and queens are called gods; but this respects their sacred power: nothing supposing an immortality attending their persons, for they all die like other men, and their dust knows no distinction in the grave. Since then it is most certain that the queen must die, and our safety and happiness in this nation depends so much upon the stability of our liberties, religion, and aforesaid dependencies after her majesty's life shall end, it cannot be a question offensive to any who has any concern in the public good, to inquire into what shall be the state of our condition, or the posture of our affairs, when the queen shall die; but this is not all neither. As the queen is mortal, and we are assured she must die, so we are none of us certain as to be able to know when, or how soon, that disaster may happen; at what time, or in what manner. This then, as it may be remote, and not a long time; God of his infinite mercy grant it may be long first, and not before this difficult question we are upon be effectually and satisfactorily answered to the nation; so on the other side, it may be near; none of us know how near, the fatal blow may befall us soon, and sooner far than we may be ready; for to-day it may come, while the cavilling reader is objecting against our putting this question, and calling it unreasonable and needless; while the word is in thy very mouth, mayest thou hear the fatal, melancholy news, the queen is dead. News that must one time or other be heard; the word will certainly come some time or other, to be spoken in the present sense, and to be sure in the time they are spoken in. How can any one then say, that it is improper to ask what shall be our case, what shall we do, or what shall be done with us, If the queen should die?

But we have another melancholy incident, which attends the queen's mortality, and which makes this question more than ordinarily seasonable to be asked at this time; and that is, that not only the queen is mortal, and she must die, and the time uncertain; so that she may die, even to-day, before to-morrow, or in a very little space of time: but her life is, under God's providence, at the mercy of papists and jacobites' people; who, the one by their principles, and the other by the circumstances of their party, are more than ordinarily to be apprehended for their bloody designs against her majesty, and against the whole nation. Nay, there seems more reason to be apprehensive of the dangerous attempts of these desperate people, at this time, than ever, even from the very reasons which are given all along in this work, for our being safe in our privileges, our religious and civil rights, during her majesty's life. It would be mispending your time to prove that the papists and jacobite parties in this nation, however they may, as we have said, be under ties and obligations of honour, interest, and gratitude, &c., not to make attempt upon us during the queen's life; yet that they are more encouraged at this time than ever they were to hope and believe, that when the queen shall die, their turn stands next. This, we say, we believe is lost labour to speak of: the said people, the popish and tory party, will freely own and oppose it. They all take their obligations to the queen to end with her majesty's life. The French king, however in honour and gratitude he may think himself bound not to encourage the pretender to insult her majesty's dominions, while the queen, with whom he personally is engaged by treaty, shall remain alive, will think himself fully at liberty from those obligations when the queen shall die. If we are not misinformed of the French affairs, and of the notions they have in France of these things, they are generally no otherwise understood than that the king of France is engaged by the peace now in view, not to disturb her majesty's possession during her reign and her life; but that then the pretender's right is to be received everywhere. The pretender himself, howsoever, as above said, he may despair of his success in attempting to take possession during the queen's life, will not fail to assume new hopes at her majesty's death: so much then of the hopes of popery and French power; so much of the interest of the pretender depending upon the single thread of life of a mortal person; and we being well assured that they look upon her majesty only as the incumbent in a living, or tenant for life in an estate, what is more natural, than in this case for us to apprehend danger to the life of the queen; especially to such people, who are known not to make much consciences of murdering princes, with whom the king-killing doctrine is so universally received, and who were so often detected of villanous practices and plots against the life of Queen Elizabeth, her majesty's famous predecessor, and that upon the same foundation, viz., the queen of Scots being the popish pretender to the crown; what can we expect from the same party, and men acting from the same principles, but the same practices? It is known that the queen, by course of nature, may live many years, and these people have many reasons to be impatient of so much delay. They know that many accidents may intervene to make the circumstances of the nation, at the time of the queen's death, less favourable to their interests than they are now; they may have fewer friends, as well in power, as out of power, by length of time, and the like: these, and such as these considerations may excite villanous and murderous practices against the precious life of our sovereign (God protect her majesty from them); but while all these considerations so naturally offer themselves to us, it seems most rational, needful, seasonable, and just, that we should be asking and answering this great question, What if the queen should die?

Thus far we have only asked the question itself, and showed our reasons, or endeavoured to justify the reasonableness of the inquiry. It follows that we make some brief essay as an answer to the question. This may be done many ways; but the design of this tract is rather to put the question into your thought, than to put an answer into your mouths. The several answers which may be given to this important question may not be proper for a public print; and some may not be fit so much as to be spoken. The question is not without its uses, whether it be answered or no, if the nation be sufficiently awakened but to ask the question among themselves; they will be brought by thinking of the thing to answer it one to another in a short space. The people of Britain want only to be showed what imminent danger they are in, in case of the queen's decease: how much their safety and felicity depend upon the life of her majesty, and what a state of confusion, distress, and all sorts of dreadful calamities they will fall into at her majesty's death, if something be not done to settle them before her death; and if they are not during her majesty's life secured from the power of France, and the danger of the pretender.

REASONS AGAINST THE SUCCESSION OF THE HOUSE of HANOVER, WITH AN ENQUIRY

How far the Abdication of King James, supposing it to be Legal, ought to affect the Person of the Pretender

What strife is here among you all? And what a noise about who shall or shall not be king, the Lord knows when? Is it not a strange thing we cannot be quiet with the queen we have, but we must all fall into confusion and combustions about who shall come after? Why, pray folks, how old is the queen, and when is she to die? that here is this pother made about it. I have heard wise people say the queen is not fifty years old, that she has no distemper but the gout, that that is a long-life disease, which generally holds people out twenty, or thirty, or forty years; and let it go how it will, the queen may well enough linger out twenty or thirty years, and not be a huge old wife neither. Now, what say the people, must we think of living twenty or thirty years in this wrangling condition we are now in? This would be a torment worse than some of the Egyptian plagues, and would be intolerable to bear, though for fewer years than that. The animosities of this nation, should they go on, as it seems they go on now, would by time become to such a height, that all charity, society, and mutual agreement among us, will be destroyed. Christians shall we be called! No; nothing of the people called Christians will be to be found among us. Nothing of Christianity, or the substance of Christianity, viz., charity, will be found among us! The name Christian may be assumed, but it will be all hypocrisy and delusion; the being of Christianity must be lost in the fog, and smoke, and stink, and noise, and rage, and cruelty, of our quarrel about a king. Is this rational? Is it agreeable to the true interest of the nation? What must become of trade, of religion, of society, of relation, of families, of people? Why, hark ye, you folk that call yourselves rational, and talk of having souls, is this a token of your having such things about you, or of thinking rationally; if you have, pray what is it likely will become of you all? Why, the strife is gotten into your kitchens, your parlours, your shops, your counting-houses, nay, into your very beds. You gentlefolks, if you please to listen to your cookmaids and footmen in your kitchens, you shall hear them scolding, and swearing, and scratching, and fighting among themselves; and when you think the noise is about the beef and the pudding, the dishwater, or the kitchen-stuff, alas, you are mistaken; the feud is about the more mighty affairs of the government, and who is for the protestant succession, and who for the pretender. Here the poor despicable scullions learn to cry, High Church, No Dutch Kings, No Hanover, that they may do it dexterously when they come into the next mob. Here their antagonists of the dripping-pan practise the other side clamour, No French Peace, No Pretender, No Popery. The thing is the very same up one pair of stairs: in the shops and warehouses the apprentices stand some on one side of the shop, and some on the other, (having trade little enough), and there they throw high church and low church at one another's heads like battledore and shuttlecock; instead of posting their books, they are fighting and railing at the pretender and the house of Hanover; it were better for us certainly that these things had never been heard of. If we go from the shop one story higher into our family, the ladies, instead of their innocent sports and diversions, they are all falling out one among another; the daughters and the mother, the mothers and the daughters; the children and the servants; nay, the very little sisters one among another. If the chambermaid is a slattern, and does not please, Hang her, she is a jade; or, I warrant she is a highflier; or, on the other side, I warrant she is a whig; I never knew one of that sort good for anything in my life. Nay, go to your very bed-chambers, and even in bed the man and wife shall quarrel about it. People! people! what will become of you at this rate? If ye cannot set man and wife together, nor your sons and daughters together, nay, nor your servants together, how will ye set your horses together, think ye? And how shall they stand together twenty or thirty years, think ye, if the queen should live so long? Before that time comes, if you are not reduced to your wits, you will be stark mad; so that unless you can find in your hearts to agree about this matter beforehand, the condition you are in, and by that time will in all likelihood be in, will ruin us all; and this is one sufficient reason why we should say nothing, and do nothing about the succession, but just let it rest where it is, and endeavour to be quiet; for it is impossible to live thus. Further, if Hanover should come while we are in such a condition, we shall ruin him, or he us, that is most certain. It remains to inquire what will be the issue of things. Why, first, if ye will preserve the succession, and keep it right, you must settle the peace of the nation: we are not in a condition to stand by the succession now, and if we go on we shall be worse able to do so; in his own strength Hanover does not pretend to come, and if he did he must miscarry: if not in his own, in whose then but the people of Britain? And if the people be a weakened, divided, and deluded people, and see not your own safety to lie in your agreement among yourselves, how shall such weak folk assist him, especially against a strong enemy; so that it will be your destruction to attempt to bring in the house of Hanover, unless you can stand by and defend him when he is come; this will make you all like Monmouth's men in the west, and you will find yourselves lifted up to halters and gibbets, not to places and preferments. Unless you reconcile yourselves to one another, and bring things to some better pass among the common people, it will be but to banter yourselves to talk of the protestant succession; for you neither will be in a condition to bring over your protestant successor, or to support him on the throne when you have brought him; and it will not be denied, but to make the attempt, and not succeed in it, is to ruin yourselves; and this I think a very good reason against the succession of the house of Hanover.

Another argument relates something to the family of Hanover itself. Here the folk are continually fighting and quarrelling with one another to such a degree as must infallibly weaken and disable the whole body of the nation, and expose them to any enemy, foreign or domestic. What prince, think you, will venture his person with a party or a faction, and that a party crushed, and under the power of their enemy; a party who have not been able to support themselves or their cause, how shall they support and defend him when he comes? And if they cannot be in a posture to defend and maintain him when they have him, how shall he be encouraged to venture himself among them? To come over and make the attempt here according to his just claim and the laws of the land, would be indeed his advantage, if there was a probability that he should succeed; otherwise the example of the king of Poland is sufficient to warn him against venturing while the nation is divided, and together by the ears, as they are here. The whole kingdom of Poland, we see, could not defend King Augustus against the Swedes and their pretender; but though he had the majority, and was received as king over the whole kingdom, yet it being a kingdom divided into factions and parties, and those parties raging with bitter envy and fury one against another, even just as ours do here, what came of it but the ruin of King Augustus, who was as it were a prisoner in his own court, and was brought to the necessity of abdicating the crown of Poland, and of acknowledging the title of the pretender to that crown. Now, what can the elector of Hanover expect, if he should make the attempt here while we are in this divided factious condition,—while the pretender, backed by his party at home, shall also have the whole power of France to support him, and place him upon the throne?

Let us but look back to a time when the very same case almost fell out in this nation; the same many ways it was, that is, in the case of Queen Mary I., your bloody papist persecuting Queen Mary and the Lady Jane Dudley, or Grey. The late King Edward VI. had settled the protestant succession upon the Lady Jane; it was received universally as the protestant succession is now. The reasons which moved the people to receive it were the same, i.e., the safety of the protestant religion, and the liberties and properties of the people; all the great men of King Edward's court and council came readily into this succession, and gave their oaths, or what was in those days (whatsoever it may be now) thought equal to an oath, viz., their honour, for the standing by the successor in her taking possession of her said just right. Mary, daughter of Catherine of Spain, was the pretender; her mother was abdicated (so we call it in this age), repudiated, they called it, or divorced. Her daughter was adjudged illegitimate or spurious, because the marriage of her mother was esteemed unlawful; just as our pretender is by this nation suggested spurious, by reason of the yet unfolded mysteries of his birth. Again, that pretender had the whole power of Spain, which was then the most dreaded of any in the world, and was just what the French are now, viz., the terror of Europe. If Queen Mary was to have the crown, it was allowed by all that England was to be governed by Spanish councils, and Spanish maxims, Spanish money, and Spanish cruelty. Just as we say now of the pretender, that if he was to come in we shall be all governed by French maxims, French councils, French money, and French tyranny. In these things the pretender (Mary) at that time was the parallel to our pretender now, and that with but very little difference. Besides all this, she was a papist, which was directly contrary to the pious design of King Edward in propagating the reformation. Exactly agreeing these things were with our succession, our pretender, our King William, and his design, by settling the succession for the propagating the revolution, which is the reformation of this day, as the reformation was the revolution of that day. After this formal settling of the succession the king (as kings and queens must) dies, and the lords of the council, as our law calls them, they were the same thing, suppose lords justices, they meet and proclaim their protestant successor, as they were obliged to do; and what followed? Had they been unanimous, had they stuck to one another, had they not divided into parties, high and low, they had kept their protestant successor in spite of all the power of Spain, but they fell out with one another; high protestants against low protestants! and what was the consequence? One side to ruin the other brought in the pretender upon them, and so Spanish power, as it was predicted, came in upon them, and devoured them all. Popery came in, as they feared, and all went to ruin; and what came of the protestant successor? Truly they brought her to ruin. For first bringing her in, and then, by reason of their own strife and divisions, not being able to maintain her in the possession of that crown, which at their request she had taken, she fell into her enemies' hand, was made a sacrifice to their fury, and brought to the block. What can be a more lively representation of our case now before us? He must have small sense of the state of our case, I think, who in our present circumstances can desire the Hanover succession should take place. What! would you bring over the family of Hanover to have them murdered? No, no, those that have a true value for the house of Hanover, would by no means desire them to come hither, or desire you to bring them on such terms; first let the world see you are in a condition to support and defend them, that the pretender, and his power and alliances of any kind, shall not disperse and ruin him and you together; first unite and put yourselves into a posture that you may defend the succession, and then you may have it; but as it stands now, good folks, consider with yourselves what prince in Europe will venture among us, and who that has any respect or value for the house of Hanover can desire them to come hither.

These are some good reasons why the succession of the house of Hanover should not be our present view. Another reason may be taken from the example of the good people in the days of King Edward VI. They were very good, religious people, that must be allowed by all sides, and who had very great zeal for the protestant religion and the reformation, as it was then newly established among them; and this zeal of theirs appeared plainly in a degree we can scarce hope for among the protestants of this age, viz., in their burning for it afterwards; yet such was their zeal for the hereditary right of their royal family, that they chose to fall into the hands of Spanish tyranny, and of Spanish popery, and let the protestant religion and the hopes of its establishment go to the d—l, rather than not have the right line of their princes kept up, and the eldest daughter of their late King Henry come to the crown. Upon this principle they forsook their good reforming King Edward's scheme, rejected the protestant succession, and they themselves, protestants, sincere protestants, such as afterwards died at a stake for their religion, the protestant religion; yet they brought in the pretender according to their principles, and run the risk of what could follow thereupon. Why should we think it strange, then, that protestants now in this age, and Church of England protestants too, should be for a popish pretender? No doubt but they may be as good protestants as the Suffolk men in Queen Mary's time were, and if they are brought to it, will go as far, and die at a stake for the protestant religion, and in doing this, no doubt, but it is their real prospect to die at a stake, or they would not do it to be sure. Now the protestant religion, the whole work of reformation, the safety of the nation, both as to their liberties and religion, the keeping out French or Spanish popery, the dying at a stake, and the like, being always esteemed things of much less value than the faithful adhering to the divine rule of keeping the crown in the right line, let any true protestant tell me, how can we pretend to be for the Hanover succession? It is evident that the divine hereditary right of our crown is the main great article now in debate. You call such a man the pretender, but is he not the son of our king? And if so, what is the protestant religion to us? Had we not much better be papists than traitors? Had we not much better deny our God, our baptism, our religion, and our lives, than deny our lawful prince, our next male in a right line? If popery comes, passive obedience is still our friend; we are protestants; we can die, we can burn, we can do anything but rebel; and this being our first duty, viz., to recognise our rightful sovereign, are we not to do that first? And if popery or slavery follow, we must act as becomes us. This being then orthodox doctrine, is equally a substantial reason why we should be against the Hanover succession.

There may be sundry other reasons given why we should not be for this new establishment of the succession, which, though perhaps they may not seem so cogent in themselves, have yet a due force, as they stand related to other circumstances, which this nation is at present involved in, and therefore are only left to the consideration of the people of these times. No question but every honest Briton is for a peaceable succession; now, if the pretender comes, and is quietly established on the throne, why then you know there is an end of all our fears of the great and formidable power of France; we have no more need to fear an invasion, or the effects of leaving France in a condition by the peace to act against us; and put the pretender upon us; and therefore, peace being of so much consequence to this nation, after so long and so cruel a war, none can think of entering upon a new war for the succession without great regret and horror. Now, it cannot be doubted but the succession of Hanover would necessarily involve us again in a war against France, and that perhaps when we may be in no good case to undertake it, for these reasons:—1. Perhaps some princes and states in the world by that time, seeing the great increase and growth of French power, may think fit to change their sentiments, and rather come over to that interest for want of being supported before, than be willing to embark against France, and so it may not be possible to obtain a new confederacy in the degree and extent of it, which we have seen it in, or in any degree suitable to the power of France; and if so, there may be but small hopes of success in case of a new rupture; and any war had better be let alone than be carried on to loss, which often ends in the overthrow of the party or nation who undertake it, and fails in the carrying it on. 2. France itself, as well by the acquisition of those princes who may have changed sides, as above, as by a time for taking breath after the losses they have received, may be raised to a condition of superior strength, and may be too much an overmatch for us to venture upon; and if he thinks fit to send us the person we call the pretender, and order us to take him for our king, and this when we are in no condition to withstand him, prudence will guide us to accept of him; for all people comply with what they cannot avoid; and if we are not in a condition to keep him out, there wants very little consultation upon the question, whether we shall take him in, or no? Like this is a man, who being condemned to be hanged, and is in irons in the dungeon at Newgate, when he sees no possibility either of pardon from the queen, or escape out of prison, what does he resolve upon next? What! why he resolves to die. What should he resolve on? Everybody submits to what they cannot escape. People! people! if ye cannot resist the French king, ye must submit to a French pretender. There is no more to be said about that. 3. Then some allies, who it might be thought would be able to lend you some help in such a case as this is, may pretend to be disgusted at former usage, and say they were abandoned and forsaken in their occasion by us, and they will not hazard for a nation who disobliged them so much before, and from whom they have not received suitable returns for the debt of the revolution. And if these nations should take things so ill as to refuse their aid and assistance in a case of so much necessity as that of the succession, how shall we be able to maintain that attempt? And, as before, an attempt of that, or any other kind like that, is better unmade than ineffectually made. 4. Others add a yet farther reason of our probable inability in such a case, viz., that the enemies of Britain have so misrepresented things to some of the neighbouring nations, our good friends and allies, as if we Britons had betrayed the protestant interest, and not acted faithfully to our confederacies and alliances, in which our reputation, it is pretended, has suffered so much, as not to merit to be trusted again in like cases, or that it should be safe to depend upon our most solemn engagements. This, though it is invidious and harsh, yet if there may be any truth in it, as we hope there is not, may be added as a very good reason, why, after this war is over, we may be in no good case at all to undertake or to carry on a new war in defence of the new protestant succession, when it may come to be necessary so to do. Since, then, the succession of Hanover will necessarily involve us in a new war against France, and for the reasons above, if they are allowed to be good reasons, we may not be in a condition to carry on that war, is not this a good reason why we should not in our present circumstances be for that succession? Other reasons may be taken from the present occasion the nation may lie under of preserving and securing the best administration of things that ever this nation was under in many ages; and if this be found to be inconsistent with the succession of Hanover, as some feign, it is hoped none will say but we ought to consider what we do; if the succession of Hanover is not consistent with these things, what reason have we to be for the said succession, till that posture of things be arrived when that inconsistency may be removed? And now, people of Britain! be your own judges upon what terms you can think it reasonable to insist any longer upon this succession. I do not contend that it is not a lawful succession, a reasonable succession, an established succession, nay, a sworn succession; but if it be not a practicable succession, and cannot be a peaceable succession; if peace will not bring him in, and war cannot, what must we do? It were much better not to have it at all, than to have it and ruin the kingdom, and ruin those that claim it at the same time.

But yet I have other reasons than these, and more cogent ones; learned men say, some diseases in nature are cured by antipathies, and some by sympathies; that the enemies of nature are the best preservatives of nature; that bodies are brought down by the skill of the physician that they may the better be brought up, made sick to be made well, and carried to the brink of the grave in order to be kept from the grave; for these reasons, and in order to these things, poisons are administered for physic;

or amputations in surgery, the flesh is cut that it may heal; an arm laid open that it may close with safety; and these methods of cure are said to be the most certain as well as most necessary in those particular cases, from whence it is become a proverbial saying in physic, desperate diseases must have desperate remedies. Now it is very proper to inquire in this case whether the nation is not in such a state of health at this time, that the coming of the pretender may not be of absolute necessity, by way of cure of such national distempers which now afflict us, and that an effectual cure can be wrought no other way? If upon due inquiry it should appear that we are not fit to receive such a prince as the successor of the house of Hanover is, that we should maltreat and abuse him if he were here, and that there is no way for us to learn the true value of a protestant successor so well as by tasting a little what a popish pretender is, and feeling something of the great advantages that may accrue to us by the superiority of a Jacobite party; if the disease of stupidity has so far seized us that we are to be cured only by poisons and fermentations; if the wound is mortified, and nothing but deep incisions, amputations, and desperate remedies must be used; if it should be necessary thus to teach us the worth of things by the want of them; and there is no other way to bring the nation to its senses; why, what can be then said against the pretender? Even let him come that we may see what slavery means, and may inquire how the chains of French galleys hang about us, and how easy wooden shoes are to walk in; for no experience teaches so well as that we buy dearest, and pay for with the most smart.

I think this may pass for a very good reason against the protestant succession; nothing is surer than that the management of King Charles II. and his late brother, were the best ways the nation could ever have taken to bring to pass the happy revolution; yet these afflictions to the island were not joyous, but grievous, for the time they remained, and the poor kingdoms suffered great convulsions; but what weighs that if these convulsions are found to be necessary to a cure? If the physicians prescribe a vomit for the cure of any particular distemper, will the patient complain of being made sick? No, no; when you begin to be sick, then we say, Oh, that is right, and then the vomit begins to work; and how shall the island of Britain spew out all the dregs and filth the public digesture has contracted, if it be not made sick with some French physic? If you give good nourishing food upon a foul stomach, you cause that wholesome food to turn into filth, and instead of nourishing the man, it nourishes diseases in the man, till those diseases prove his destruction, and bring him to the grave. In like manner, if you will bring the protestant successor into the government before that government have taken some physic to cleanse it from the ill digesture it may have been under, how do we know but the diseases which are already begun in the constitution may not be nourished and kept up, till they may hereafter break out in the days of our posterity, and prove mortal to the nation. Wherefore should we desire the protestant successor to come in upon a foot of high-flying menage, and be beholden for their establishment to those who are the enemies of the constitution? Would not this be to have in time to come the successors of that house be the same thing as the ages passed have already been made sick of, and made to spew out of the government? Are not any of these considerations enough to make any of us averse to the protestant succession? No, no; let us take a French vomit first, and make us sick, that we may be well, and may afterwards more effectually have our health established.

The pretender will no doubt bring us good medicines, and cure us of all our hypochondriac vapours that now make us so giddy. But, say some, he will bring popery in upon us; popery, say you! alas! it is true, popery is a sad thing, and that, say some folk, ought to have been thought on before now; but suppose then this thing called popery! How will it come in? Why, say the honest folk, the pretender is a papist, and if a popish prince come upon the throne we shall have popery come in upon us without fail. Well, well, and what hurt will this be to you? May not popery be very good in its kind? What if this popery, like the vomit made of poison, be the only physic that can cure you? If this vomit make you spew out your filth, your tory filth, your idolatrous filth, your tyrannic filth, and restore you to your health, shall it not be good for you? Where pray observe in the allegory of physic; you heard before when you take a vomit, the physic given you to vomit is always something contrary to nature, something that if taken in quantity would destroy; but how does it operate? It attacks nature, and puts her upon a ferment to cast out what offends her; but remark it, I pray, when the patient vomits, he always vomits up the physic and the filth together; so, if the nation should take a vomit of popery, as when the pretender comes most certain it is that this will be the consequence, they will vomit up the physic and the filth together; the popery and the pretender will come all up again, and all the popish, arbitrary, tyrannical filth, which has offended the stomach of the nation so long, and ruined its digesture, it will all come up together; one vomit of popery will do us all a great deal of good, for the stomach of the constitution is marvellous foul. Observe, people! this is no new application; the nation has taken a vomit of this kind before now, as in Queen Mary I.'s time; the reformation was not well chewed, and being taken down whole, did not rightly digest, but left too much crudity in the stomach, from whence proceeded ill nourishment, bad blood, and a very ill habit of body in the constitution; witness the distemper which seized the Gospellers in Suffolk, who being struck with an epilepsy or dead palsy in the better half of their understanding, to wit, the religious and zealous part, took up arms for a popish pretender, against the protestant successor, upon the wild-headed whimsey of the right line being jure divino. Well, what followed, I pray? Why, they took a vomit of popery; the potion indeed was given in a double vehicle, viz., of fagots a little inflamed, and this worked so effectually, that the nation having vomited, brought up all the filth of the stomach, and the foolish notion of hereditary right, spewed out popery also along with it. Thus was popery, and fire and fagot, the most effectual remedy to cure the nation of all its simple diseases, and to settle and establish the protestant reformation; and why then should we be so terrified with the apprehensions of popery? Nay, why should we not open our eyes and see how much to our advantage it may be in the next reign to have popery brought in, and to that end the pretender set up, that he may help us to this most useful dose of physic? These are some other of my reasons against the protestant succession; I think they cannot be mended; it may perhaps be thought hard of that we should thus seem to make light of so terrible a thing as popery, and should jest with the affair of the protestants; no, people! no; this is no jest,—taking physic is no jest at all; for it is useful many ways, and there is no keeping the body in health without it; for the corruption of politic constitutions are as gross and as fatal as those of human bodies, and require as immediate application of medicines. And why should you people of this country be so alarmed, and seem so afraid of this thing called popery, when it is spoken of in intelligible terms, since you are not afraid alternately to put your hands to those things which as naturally tend in themselves to bring it upon you, as clouds tend to rain, or smoke to fire; what does all your scandalous divisions, your unchristian quarrellings, your heaping up reproaches, and loading each other with infamy, and with abominable forgeries, what do these tend to but to popery? If it should be asked how have these any such reference? the question is most natural from the premises. If divisions weaken the nation; if whig and tory, even united, are, and have been, weak enough to keep out popery, surely then widening the unnatural breaches, and inflaming things between them to implacable and irreconcileable breaches, must tend to overthrow the protestant kingdom, which, as our ever blessed Saviour said, when divided against itself cannot stand. Besides, are not your breaches come up to that height already as to let any impartial bystander see that popery must be the consequences? Do not one party say openly, they had rather be papists than presbyterians; that they would rather go to mass than to a meeting-house; and are they not to that purpose, all of them who are of that height, openly joined with the jacobites in the cause of popery? On the other hand, are not the presbyterians in Scotland so exasperated at having the abjuration oath imposed upon them, contrary, as they tell us, to their principles, that they care not if he, or any else, would come now and free them from that yoke? What is all this but telling us plainly that the whole nation is running into popery and the pretender? Why then, while you are obliquely, and by consequences, joining your hands to bring in popery, why, O distracted folk! should you think it amiss to have me talk of doing it openly and avowedly? Better is open enmity than secret guile; better is it to talk openly, and profess openly, for popery, that you may see the shape and real picture of it, than pretend strong opposition of it, and be all at the same time putting your hands to the work, and pulling it down upon yourselves with all your might.

But here comes an objection in our way, which, however weighty, we must endeavour to get over, and this is, what becomes of the abjuration? If the pretender comes in we are all perjured, and we ought to be all unanimous for the house of Hanover, because we are all perjured if we are for the pretender. Perjured, say ye! Ha! why, do all these people say we are perjured already? Nay, one, two, three, or four times? What signify oaths and abjurations in a nation where the parliament can make an oath to-day, and punish a man for keeping it to-morrow! Besides, taking oaths without examination, and breaking them without consideration, hath been so much a practice, and the date of its original is so far back, that none, or but very few, know where to look for it; nay, have we not been called in the vulgar dialect of foreign countries "the swearing nation"? Note, we do not say the forsworn nation; for whatever other countries say of us, it is not meet we should say so of ourselves; but as to swearing and forswearing, associating and abjuring, there are very few without sin to throw the first stone, and therefore we may be the less careful to answer in this matter: it is evident that the friends of the pretender cannot blame us; for have not the most professed jacobites all over the nation taken this abjuration? Nay, when even in their hearts they have all the while resolved to be for the pretender? Not to instance in the swearing in all ages to and against governments, just as they were or were not, in condition to protect us, or keep others out of possession; but we have a much better way to come off this than that, and we doubt not to clear the nation of perjury, by declaring the design, true intent, and meaning of the thing itself; for the good or evil of every action is said to lie in the intention; if then we can prove the bringing in the pretender to be done with a real intention and sincere desire to keep him out, or, as before, to spew him out; if we bring in popery with an intention and a sincere design to establish the protestant religion; if we bring in a popish prince with a single design the firmer and better to fix and introduce the protestant Hanover succession; if, I say, these things are the true intent and meaning, and are at the bottom of all our actions in this matter, pray how shall we be said to be perjured, or to break in upon the abjuration, whose meaning we keep, whatever becomes of the literal part of it. Thus we are abundantly defended from the guilt of perjury, because we preserve the design and intention upright and entire for the house of Hanover; though as the best means to bring it to pass we think fit to bring in popery and the pretender: but yet farther, to justify the lawfulness and usefulness of such kind of methods, we may go back to former experiments of the same case, or like cases, for nothing can illustrate such a thing so aptly, as the example of eminent men who have practised the very same things in the same or like cases, and more especially when that practice has been made use of by honest men in an honest cause, and the end been crowned with success. This eminent example was first put in practice by the late famous Earl of Sunderland, in the time of King James II., and that too in the case of bringing popery into England, which is the very individual article before us. This famous politician, if fame lies not, turned papist himself, went publicly to mass, advised and directed all the forward rash steps that King James afterwards took towards the introducing of popery into the nation; if he is not slandered, it was he advised the setting up of popish chapels and mass-houses in the city of London, and in the several principal towns of this nation; the invading the right of corporations, courts of justice, universities, and, at last, the erecting the high commission court, to sap the foundations of the church; and many more of the arbitrary steps which that monarch took for the ruin of the protestant religion, as he thought, were brought about by this politic earl, purely with design, and as the only effectual means to ruin the popish schemes, and bring about the establishment of the protestant religion by the revolution; and, as experience after made it good, he alone was in the right, and it was the only way left, the only step that could be taken, though at first it made us all of the opinion the man was going the ready way to ruin his country, and that he was selling us to popery and Rome. This was exactly our case;

the nation being sick of a deadly, and otherwise incurable disease, this wise physician knew that nothing but a medicine made up of deadly poison, that should put the whole body into convulsions, and make it cast up the dregs of the malady, would have any effect; and so he applied himself accordingly to such a cure; he brought on popery to the very door; he caused the nation to swallow as much of it as he thought was enough to make her as sick as a horse, and then he foresaw she would spew up the disease and the medicine together; the potion of popery he saw would come up with it, and so it did. If this be our case now, then it may be true that bringing the pretender is the only way to establish the protestant succession; and upon such terms, and such only, I declare myself for the pretender. If any sort of people are against the succession of the house of Hanover on any other accounts, and for other reasons, it may not be amiss to know some of them, and a little to recommend them to those who have a mind to be for him, but well know not wherefore or why they are so inclined. 1. Some being instructed to have an aversion to all foreign princes or families, are against the succession of the princes of Hanover, because, as they are taught to say, they are Dutchmen; now, though it might as well be said of the pretender that he is a Frenchman, yet that having upon many accounts been made more familiar to them of late, and the name of a Dutch king having a peculiar odium left upon it, by the grievances of the late King William's reign, they can by no means think of another Dutch succession without abhorrence; nay, the aversion is so much greater than their aversions to popery, that they can with much more satisfaction entertain the notion of a popish French pretender than of the best protestant in the world, if he hath anything belonging to him that sounds like a Dutchman; and this is some people's reason against the Hanover succession; a reason which has produced various effects in the world since the death of that prince, even to creating national antipathies in some people to the whole people of Holland, and to wish us involved in a war with the Dutch without any foundation of a quarrel with them, or any reason for those aversions; but these things opening a scene which relates to things farther back than the subject we are now upon, we omit them here for brevity sake, and to keep more closely to the thing in hand at this time. Others have aversions to the Hanover succession as it is the effect of the revolution, and as it may reasonably be supposed to favour such principles as the revolution was brought about by, and has been the support of, viz., principles of liberty, justice, rights of parliaments, the people's liberties, free possession of property, and such like; these doctrines, a certain party in this nation have always to their utmost opposed, and have given us reason to believe they hate and abhor them, and for this reason they cannot be supposed to appear forward for the Hanover succession; to these principles have been opposed the more famous doctrines of passive obedience, absolute will, indefeasible right, the jus divinum of the line of princes, hereditary right, and such like; these, as preached up by that eminent divine, Dr. Henry Sacheverell, are so much preferable to the pretences of liberty and constitution, the old republican notions of the whigs, that they cannot but fill these people with hatred against all those that would pretend to maintain the foundation we now stand upon, viz., the revolution; and this is their reason against the Hanover succession, which they know would endeavour to do so.

Come we in the conclusion of this great matter to one great and main reason, which they say prevails with a great part of the nation at this time to be for the pretender, and which many subtle heads and industrious hands are now busily employed all over the kingdom to improve in the minds of the common people, this is the opinion of the legitimacy of the birth of the pretender; it seems, say these men, that the poor commons of Britain have been all along imposed upon to believe that the person called the pretender was a spurious birth, a child fostered upon the nation by the late king and queen; this delusion was carried on, say they, by the whigs in King William's time, and a mighty stir was made of it to possess the rabbles in favour of the revolution, but nothing was ever made of it; King William, say they, promised in his declaration to have it referred to the decision of the English parliament, but when he obtained the crown he never did anything that way more than encourage the people to spread the delusion by scurrilous pamphlets to amuse the poor commons; have them take a thing for granted which could have no other thing made of it; and so the judging of it in parliament was made a sham only; and the people drinking in the delusion, as they who were in the plot desired, it has passed ever since as if the thing had been sufficiently proved. Now upon a more sedate considering the matter, say they, the case is clear that this person is the real son of King James, and the favourers of the revolution go now upon another foundation, viz., the powers of parliaments to limit the succession; and that succession being limited upon King James's abdication, which they call voluntary; so that now, say they, the question about the legitimacy of the person called the pretender is over, and nothing now is to be said of it; that he is the son of King James, there is, say they, no more room to doubt, and therefore the doctrine of hereditary right taking place, as the ancient professed doctrine of the Church of England, there can be no objection against his being our lawful king; and it is contrary to the said Church of England doctrine to deny it. This, then, is the present reason which the poor ignorant people are taught to give why they are against the protestant succession, and why they are easily persuaded to come into the new scheme of a popish pretender, though at the same time they are all heartily against popery as much as ever.

It becomes necessary now to explain this case a little to the understanding of the common people, and let them know upon what foundation the right of these two parties is founded, and if this be done with plainness and clearness, as by the rights and laws of Englishmen and Britons appertaineth, the said commons of Britain may soon discover whether the succession of the house of Hanover, or the claim of the person called the pretender, is founded best, and which they ought to adhere unto. The first thing it seems to be made clear to the common people is, whether the pretender was the lawful son of King James, yea, or no? And why the contrary to this was not made appear, according to the promises which, they say, though falsely, were made by the late King William? In the first place is to be considered, that the declaration of the said king, when P. of O. putting the said case in the modestest manner possible, had this expression, That there were violent suspicions that the said person was not born of the queen's body, and that the prince resolved to leave the same to the free parliament, to which throughout the said declaration the said prince declared himself ready to refer all the grievances which he came over to redress. I shall give you this in the words of a late learned author upon that head.

That before a free parliament could be obtained, King James withdrew himself, and carried away his pretended son into the hands of the ancient enemies of this nation, and of our religion, viz., the French, there to be educated in the principles of enmity to this his native country.

By which action he not only declined to refer the legitimacy of his said son to the examination of the parliament, as the Prince of Orange had offered in his said declaration, but made such examination altogether useless and impracticable, he himself (King James) not owning it to be a legal parliament, and therefore not consenting to stand by such examination.

By the said abdication, and carrying away his said pretended son into the hands of the French to be educated in popery, &c., he gave the parliament of England and Scotland abundant reason for ever to exclude the said King James and his said pretended son from the government of these realms, or from the succession to the same, and made it absolutely necessary for them to do so, if they would secure the protestant religion to themselves and their posterity; and this without any regard to the doubt, whether he was the lawful son of King James, or no, since it is inconsistent with the constitution of this protestant nation to be governed by a popish prince.

The proof of the legitimacy being thus stated, and all the violent suspicions of his not being born of the queen being thus confirmed by the abdication of King James, come we next to examine how far this abdication could forfeit for this pretender, supposing him to be the real son of King James; this returns upon the right of the parliament to limit the succession, supposing King James had had no son at all; if the abdication be granted a lawfully making the throne vacant, it will be very hard to assign a cause why the parliament might not name a successor while the father was alive, whose right had no violent suspicions attending it, and not why they might not name a successor though the son was living; that the father's abdication forfeited for the son is no part of the question before us; for the father is not said to forfeit his right at all; no one ever questioned his right to reign, nor, had he thought fit to have stayed, could the parliament have named a successor, unless, as in the case of Richard II., he had made a voluntary resignation or renunciation of the crown, and of his people's allegiance; but the king having voluntarily abdicated the throne, this was as effectual a releasing his subjects from their allegiance to him, as if he had read an instrument of resignation, just as King Richard did; all the articles of such a resignation were naturally contained in the said abdication, except the naming the successor, as effectually as if they had been at large repeated; and since the resigning the crown has been formerly practised in England, and there is so eminent an example in our English history of the same, it will questionless be of use to the reader of these sheets to have the particulars of it before his eyes, which for that purpose is here set down at large, as it was done in the presence of a great number of English peers, who attended the king for that purpose, and is as follows:—

In the name of God, Amen. I Richard, by the grace of God, King of England and France, and Lord of Ireland, do hereby acquit and discharge all Archbishops, Bishops, Dukes, Marquisses, and Earls, Barons, Lords, and all other my subjects, both spiritual and secular, of what degree soever, from their oath of fealty and homage, and all other bonds of allegiance, to me due from them and their heirs, and do hereby release them from the said oath and allegiance, so far as they concern my person, for ever.

I also resign all my kingly majesty and dignity, with all the rights and privileges thereunto belonging, and do renounce all the title and claim which I ever had, or have, to them. I also renounce the government of the said kingdom, and the name and royal highness thereunto belonging, freely and wholly, and swearing upon the Evangelists that I will never oppose this my voluntary resignation, nor suffer it to be opposed, as judging myself not unworthily deposed from my regal dignity for my deserts.

This resignation being read again in parliament, they grounded the deposing King Richard upon it, and declared him accordingly deposed, that is, declared the throne vacant; and immediately, by virtue of their own undoubted right of limiting the succession, named the successor. See the form in the history of that time, thus:—

That the throne was vacant by the voluntary cession and just deposition of King Richard II., and that therefore, according to their undoubted power and right so to do, they ought forthwith to the naming a successor to fill the said throne, which they forthwith did, by naming and proclaiming Henry, Duke of Lancaster, to be king, &c.

See the history of the kings of England, vol. fol. 287.

This was the same thing with King James's abdication, and King James's abdication was no less or more than an effectual resignation in form; now the parliament, upon the resignation of the crown by the king, having a manifold and manifest right to supply the throne so become vacant, had no obligation to regard the posterity of the abdicated prince, so far as any of them are concerned in, or involved by, the said abdication, and therefore considered of establishing and limiting the succession, without mentioning the reasons of the descent, having the reasons in themselves; but suppose the son of King

James had been allowed legitimate, yet as the father had involved him in the same circumstances with himself, by first carrying him out of the kingdom, and afterwards educating him in the popish religion, he became abdicated also with his father; neither doth the being voluntary or not voluntary alter the case in the least, since in the laws of England a father is allowed to be able to forfeit for himself and for his children, and much more may he make a resignation for himself and his children, as is daily practised and allowed in law in the cutting off entails and remainders, even when the heir entail is in being, and under age. The people of Britain ought not then to suffer themselves to be imposed upon in such a case; for though the pretender were to be owned for the lawful son of King James, yet the abdication of King James his father, and especially his own passive abdication, was as effectual an abdication in him as if he had been of age, and done it voluntarily himself, and shall be allowed to be as binding in all respects in law as an heir in possession cutting off an heir entail. If this is not so, then was the settlement of the crown upon King William and Queen Mary unrighteous, and those two famous princes must be recorded in history for parricides and usurpers; nor will it end there, for the black charge must reach our most gracious sovereign, who must be charged with the horrible crimes of robbery and usurpation; and not the parliament or convention of the estates at the revolution only shall be charged as rebels and traitors to their sovereign, and breakers of the great command of rendering to Cæsar the things that are Cæsar's, but even every parliament since, especially those who have had any hand in placing the entail of the crown upon the person of the queen, and in confirming her majesty's possession thereof since her happy accession; and every act of parliament settling the succession on the house of Hanover must have likewise been guilty of treason and rebellion in a most unnatural manner. This is a heavy charge upon her majesty, and very inconsistent with the great zeal and affection with which all the people of Britain at this time pay their duty and allegiance to her majesty's person, and acknowledge her happy government; this may indeed be thought hard, but it is evident nothing less can be the case, and therefore those people who are so forward to plead the pretender's cause, on account of his being King James's lawful son, can do it upon no other terms than these, viz., to declare that the queen is herself an illegal governor, an usurper of another's right, and therefore ought to be deposed; or, that the hereditary right of princes is no indefeasible thing, but is subjected to the power of limitations by parliament. Thus I think the great difficulty of the pretender's being the rightful son of the late King James is over, and at an end; that it is no part of the needful inquiry relating to the succession, since his father involved him in the fate of his abdication, and many ways rendered him incapable to reign, and out of condition to have any claim; since the power of limiting the succession to the crown is an undoubted right of the parliaments of England and of Scotland respectively. Moreover, his being educated a papist in France, and continuing so, was a just reason why the people of England rejected him, and why they ought to reject him, since, according to that famous vote of the commons in the convention parliament, so often printed, and so often on many accounts quoted, it is declared, That it is inconsistent with the constitution of this protestant kingdom to be governed by a popish prince. Vid. Votes of the Convention, Feb. 2nd, 1688. This vote was carried up by Mr. Hampden to the house of lords the same day as the resolution of all the commons of England. Now, this prince being popish, not only so in his infancy, but continuing so even now, when all the acts of Parliament in Britain have been made to exclude him, his turning protestant now, which his emissaries promise for him, though perhaps without his consent, will not answer at all; for the acts of parliament, or some of them, having been past while he, though of age, remained a papist, and gave no room to expect any other, his turning protestant cannot alter those laws, suppose he should do so; nor is it reasonable that a nation should alter an established succession to their crown whenever he shall think fit to alter or change his religion; if to engage the people of Britain to settle the succession upon him, and receive him as heir, he had thought fit to turn protestant, why did he not declare himself ready to do so before the said succession was settled by so many laws, especially by that irrevocable law of the union of the two kingdoms, and that engagement of the abjuration, of which no human power can absolve us, no act of parliament can repeal it, nor no man break it without wilful perjury.

What, then, is the signification to the people of Britain whether the person called the pretender be legitimate, or no? The son of King James, or the son of a cinder-woman? The case is settled by the queen, by the legislative authority, and we cannot go back from it; and those who go about as emissaries to persuade the commons of Great Britain of the pretender having a right, go about at the same time traitorously to tell the queen's good subjects that her majesty is not our rightful queen, but an usurper.

AN HUMBLE PROPOSAL TO THE PEOPLE OF ENGLAND, FOR THE INCREASE OF THEIR TRADE, AND ENCOURAGEMENT OF MANUFACTURES; WHETHER THE PRESENT UNCERTAINITY OF AFFAIRS ISSUES IN PEACE OR WAR

PREFACE TO THE PEOPLE OF ENGLAND

It deserves some notice, that just at, or soon after writing these sheets, we have an old dispute warmly revived among us, upon the question of our trade being declined, or not declined. I have nothing to do with the parties, nor with the reason of their strife upon that subject; I think they are wrong on both sides, and yet it is hardly worth while to set them to rights, their quarrel being quite of another nature, and the good of our trade little or nothing concerned in it.

Nor do they seem to desire to be set right, but rather to want an occasion to keep up a strife which perhaps serves some other of their wicked purposes, better than peace would do; and indeed, those who seek to quarrel, who can reconcile?

I meddle not with the question, I say, whether trade be declined or not; but I may easily show the people of England, that if they please to concern themselves a little for its prosperity, it will prosper; and on the contrary, if they will sink it and discourage it, it is evidently in their power, and it will sink and decline accordingly.

You have here some popular mistakes with respect to our woollen manufacture fairly stated, our national indolence in that very particular reproved, and the consequence laid before you; if you will not make use of the hints here given, the fault is nobody's but your own.

Never had any nation the power of improving their trade, and of advancing their own manufactures, so entirely in their own hands as we have at this time, and have had for many years past, without troubling the legislature about it at all: and though it is of the last importance to the whole nation, and, I may say, to almost every individual in it; nay, and that it is evident you all know it to be so; yet how next to impossible is it to persuade any one person to set a foot forward towards so great and so good a work; and how much labour has been spent in vain to rouse us up to it?

The following sheets are as one alarm more given to the lethargic age, if possible, to open their eyes to their own prosperity; the author sums up his introduction to it in this short positive assertion, which he is ready to make good, viz., That if the trade of England is not in a flourishing and thriving condition, the fault and only occasion of it is all our own, and is wholly in our own power to mend, whenever we please.

As by my title I profess to be addressing myself to Englishmen, I think I need not tell them that they live by trade; that their commerce has raised them from what they were to what they are, and may, if cultivated and improved, raise them yet further to what they never were; and this in few words is an index of my present work.

It is worth an Englishman's remark, that we were esteemed as a growing thriving nation in trade as far back as in the reigns of the two last Henries; manufactures were planted, navigation increased, the people began to apply, and trade bringing in wealth, they were greatly encouraged; yet in king Henry VIII.'s reign, and even towards the latter end of it, too, we find several acts of parliament passed for regulating the price of provisions, and particularly that beef and pork should not be sold in the market for more than a halfpenny per pound avoirdupoise, and mutton and veal at three farthings.

As the trading men to whom I write may make some estimate of things by calculating one thing by another, so this leads them to other heads of trade to calculate from; as, first, the value of money, which bore some proportion, though I think not a full and just equality to the provisions, as follows:—silver was at 2s. 4d. per ounce, and gold at 2l. 5s. to 2l. 10s. per ounce; something less in the silver, and more in the gold than half of the present value.

As for the rate of lands and houses, they bore a yet greater distance in value from what they produce now; so that indeed it bears no proportion, for we find the rent of lands so raised, and their value so improved, that there are many examples where the lands, valued even in queen Elizabeth's days at £20 to £25 per annum, are now worth from £200-300 per annum, and in some places much more.

It is true, this advance is to be accounted for by the improvement made of the soil, by manuring, cultivating, and enclosing; by stocks of cattle, by labour, and by the arts of husbandry, which are also improved; and so this part is not so immediately within my present design; it is a large subject, and merits to be spoken of at large by itself; because as the improvement of land has been extraordinary great, and the landed interest is prodigiously increased by it, so it is capable of much more and greater improvement than has been made for above a hundred years past. But this I say is not my present design; it is too great an article to be couched in a few words.

Yet it requires this notice here; viz., that trade has been a principal agent even in the improvement of our land; as it has furnished the money to the husbandman to stock his land, and to employ servants and labourers in the working part; and as it has found him a market for the consumption of the produce of his land, and at an advanced price too, by which he has received a good return to enable him to go on.

The short inference from these premises is this: as by trade the whole kingdom is thus advanced in wealth, and the value of lands, and of the produce of lands, and of labour, is so remarkably increased, why should we not go on with vigour and spirit in trade, and by all proper and possible methods and endeavours, increase and cultivate our commerce; that we may still increase and improve in wealth, in value of lands, in stock, and in all the arts of trade, such as manufactures, navigation, fishery, husbandry, and, in short, study an improvement of trade in all its branches.

No doubt it would be our wisdom to do thus; and nothing of the kind can be more surprising than that it should not be our practice; and thus I am brought down to the case before me.

If it should be objected that the remark is needless, that we are an industrious and laborious people, that we are the best manufacturers in the world, thoroughly versed in all the methods and arts for that purpose; and that our trade is improved to the utmost in all places, and all cases possible; if it should, I say, be thus argued, for I know some have such a taint of our national vanity that they do talk at this rate,—

My answer is short, and direct in the negative; and I do affirm that we are not that industrious, applying, improving people that we pretend to be, and that we ought to be, and might be. That we are the best manufacturers I deny; and yet at the same time I grant that we make the best manufactures in the world; but the reason of that is greatly owing not to our own skill exceeding others, so much as to our being furnished from the bounty of Heaven with the best materials and best conveniencies for the work, of any nation in the world, of which I shall take notice in its place.

But not to dwell upon our capacities for improving in trade, I might clear all that part without giving up the least article of my complaint; for it is not our capacity to improve that I call in question, but our application to the right methods; nay, I must add, that while I call upon your diligence, and press you to application, I am supposed to grant your capacities; otherwise I was calling upon you to no purpose, and pressing you to do what at the same time I allowed you had no power to perform.

Without complimenting your national vanity, therefore, I am to grant you have not only the means of improvement in your hands, but the capacity of improving also; and on this account I must add, are the more inexcusable if the thing is not in practice.

Indeed it is something wonderful, and not easy to be accounted for, that a whole nation should, as if they were in a lethargic dream, shut their eyes to the apparent advantages of their commerce; and this just now, when their circumstances seem so evidently to stand in need of encouragement, and that they are more than ordinarily at a kind of stop in their usual progression of trade.

It is debated much among men of business, whether trade is at this time in a prosperous and thriving condition, or in a languishing and declining state; or, in a word, whether we are going backwards or forward. I shall not meddle with that debate here, having no occasion to take up the little space allowed me in anything remote from my design. But I will propose it as I really believe it to be: namely, that we are rather in a state of balance between both, a middle between the extremes; I hope we are not much declined, and I fear we are not much advanced. But I must add, that if we do not immediately set about some new methods for altering this depending condition, we shall soon decline; and on the contrary, if we should exert ourselves, we have before us infinite advantages of improving and advancing our commerce, and that to a great degree.

This is stating it to the meanest understanding; there is no mystery at all in the thing; if you will apply, you will rise; if you will remain indolent and inactive, you will sink and starve. Trade in England, at this time, is like a ship at sea, that has sprung a leak in sight of the shore, or within a few days' sail of it; if the crew will ply their pump and work hard, they may not only keep her above water, but will bring her safe into port; whereas if they neglect the pump, or do not exert their strength, the water grows upon them and they are in apparent danger of sinking before they reach the shore.

Or, if you will have a coarser comparison, take the pump room in the rasp-house, or house of correction, at Amsterdam; where the slothful person is put into a good, dry, and wholesome room, with a pump at one side and a spring or water-pipe at the other; if he pleases to work, he may live and keep the water down, but if he sleeps he drowns.

The moral is exactly the same in both cases, and suits with the present circumstances of our trade in England most exactly, only with this difference to the advantage of the latter; namely, that the application which I call upon the people of England to exert themselves in, is not a mere labour of the hand; I do not tax the poor with mere sloth and negligence, idly lying still when they should work, that is not our grievance at present; for though there may be too much of that sort too, among a few of the drunken, loitering part of mankind, and they suffer for it sufficiently in their poverty, yet that, I say, is not the point, idleness is not here a national crime, the English are not naturally a slothful, indolent, or lazy people.

But it is an application proper to the method of business which is wanting among us, and in this we shall find room for reproof on one hand, and direction on the other; and our reader, I dare say, will acknowledge there is reason for both.

It must in the first place be acknowledged, that England has indeed the greatest encouragement for their industry of any nation in Europe; and as therefore their want of improving those advantages and encouragements, lays them more open to our just reproof, than other nation's would be, or can be who want them, so it moves me with the more importunity to press home the argument, which reason and the nature of the thing furnishes, to persuade them. Reason dictates that no occasion should be let slip by which England above all nations in the world should improve the advantages they have in their hands; not only because they have them, but because their people so universally depend upon them. The manufactures are their bread, the life, the comfort of their poor, and the soul of their trade; nature dictates, that as they are given them to improve, and that by industry and application they are capable of being improved; so they ought to starve if they do not improve them to the utmost.

Let us see in a few words what nature and providence has done for us; nay, what they have done for us exclusive of the rest of the world. The bounty of Heaven has stored us with the principles of commerce, fruitful of a vast variety of things essential to trade, and which call upon us as it were in the voice of nature, bidding us work, and with annexed encouragement to do so from the visible apparent success of industry. Here the voice of the world is plain, like the answer of an oracle; thus, dig and find, plough and reap, fish and take, spin and live; in a word, trade and thrive; and this with such extraordinary circumstances, that it is as if there was a bar upon the neighbouring nations, and it had been spoken from Heaven thus: These are for you only, and not for any other nation; you, my favourites, of England; you, singled out to be great, opulent, powerful, above all your neighbours, and to be made so by your own industry and my bounty.

To explain this, allow me a small digression, to run over the detail of Heaven's bounty, and see what God and nature has done for us beyond what it has done for other nations; nature, as I have said, will dictate to us what Heaven expects from us, for the improving the blessings bestowed, and for making ourselves that rich and powerful people which he has determined us to be.

Our country is furnished, I say, with the principles of commerce in a very extraordinary manner; that is to say, so as no other country in Europe, or perhaps in the world, is supplied with.

I. With the product of the earth. This is of two kinds: 1. That of the inside or bowels of the earth, the same of which, as above, the voice of Heaven to us, is, dig and find, under which article is principally our lead, and tin-coal; I name these only, because of these this island seems to have an exclusive grant; there being none, or but very small quantities of them, found in any other nation; and it is upon exclusive benefits that I am chiefly speaking. 2. We have besides these, iron, copper, lapis calaminaris, vulgarly called callamy, with several other minerals, which may be said to be in common to us and the rest of the world, of which the particulars at large, and the places where they are found, may be fully seen in a late tract, of which I shall have frequently occasion to speak in this work, entitled, A Plan of the Commerce of Great Britain, to which I refer, as indeed to a general index of the trade and produce of this whole island.

II. The product of the surface, which I include in that part, plough and reap; and though this is not indeed an exclusive product, yet I may observe that the extraordinary increase which our lands, under an excellent cultivation, generally yield, as well in corn and cattle, is an uncommon argument for the industry of the husbandmen; and I might enter into a comparison with advantage, against almost any countries in Europe, by comparing the quantity produced on both sides, with the quantity of land which produce those quantities.

You may find some calculations of the produce of our own country in the book above mentioned, viz., The Plan of the Commerce of Great Britain, where the consumption of malt in England is calculated by the value of the duties of excise, and where it appears that there is annually consumed in England, besides what is exported to foreign countries, forty millions of bushels of malt, besides also all the barley, the meal of which is made into bread, which is a very great quantity; most of the northern counties in England feeding very much upon barley bread; and besides all the barley either exported or used at home in the corn unmalted; all which put together, I am assured, amounts to no less than ten millions of bushels more.

The quantity of barley only is so exceeding great, that I am told it bears, in proportion to the land it grows on, an equality to as much land in France, as all the sowed land in the whole kingdom of England; or take it thus, that fifty millions of bushels of barley growing in France, would take up as much ground as all the lands which are at any time sowed in England with any corn, whether barley, oats, or wheat.

N. B. I do not say all the arable lands of England, because we know there are a very great number of acres of land which every year lie fallow (though in tillage) and unsowed, according to the usage of our husbandry; so they cannot be reckoned to produce any corn at all, otherwise the quantity might be much greater.

This is a testimony of the fertility of our soil; and on the other hand, the fertility is a testimony of the diligence and application of our people, and the success which attends that diligence.

We are told that in some parts of England, especially in the counties of Essex, Hertford, Cambridge, Bedford, Bucks, Oxford, Northampton, Lincoln, and Nottingham, it is very frequent to have the lands produce from seven to ten quarters of barley upon an acre, which is a produce not heard of in the most fruitful of all those we call corn countries abroad, much less in France. On the contrary, if they have a great produce of corn, it is because they have a vast extent of land for it to grow upon, and which land they either have no other use for, or it may be is fit for no other use; whereas our corn grounds are far from being the richest or the best of our lands, the prime of our land being laid up, as the ploughmen call it, to feed upon, that is, to keep dairies of cows, as in Essex, Suffolk, and the fens; or for grazing grounds, for fatting the large mutton and beef, for which England is so particularly famed. These grazing countries are chiefly in Sussex, and in the marshes of Romney, and other parts in Kent; also in the rich vales of Aylesbury, and others in Bucks and Berkshire, the isle of Ely, the bank of Trent, the counties of Lincoln, Leicester and Stafford, Warwick and Chester, as also in the county of Somerset, Lancaster, north riding of Yorkshire, and bank of Tees, in the bishoprick of Durham.

When this product of England is considered, the diligence and success of our husbandry in England will be found to be beyond that of the most industrious people in Europe. But I must not dwell here, my view lies another way; nor do the people of England want so much to be called upon to improve in husbandry, as they do in manufactures and other things; not but that even in this, the lands not yet cultivated do call aloud upon us too; but I say it is not the present case.

I come in the next article to that yet louder call of the oracle, as above, namely, fish and take. Indeed this is an improvement not fully preserved, or a produce not sufficiently improved; the advantages nature offers here cannot be said to be fully accepted of and embraced.

This is a large field, and much remains to be said and done too in it, for the increase of wealth, and the employment of our people; and though I am not of the opinion which some have carried to an unaccountable length in this case, viz., that we should set up the fishery by companies and societies, which has been often attempted, and has proved abortive and ill-grounded; or that we ought by force, or are able by all our advantages to beat out the Dutch from it; yet we might certainly very much enlarge and increase our own share in it; take greater quantities than we do; cure and pack them better than we do; come sooner to market with them than we do; and consume greater quantities at home than we do; the consequence of which would be that we should breed up and employ more seamen, build and fit out more fishing-vessels and ships for merchandise than we do now, and which we are unaccountably blameable that we do not.

And here I must observe, that the increasing the fishery would even contribute to our vending as well as catching a greater quantity of fish, and to take off the disadvantage which we now lie under with the Dutch, by the consequence of trade in the fishery itself. The case is this: the chief market for white herring, which is the fishery I am speaking of, is the port of Dantzic and Konigsberg, from which ports the whole kingdom of Poland, and great duchy of Lithuania, are supplied with fish by the navigation of the great river of the Vistula, and the smaller rivers of the Pragel and Niemen, &c.

The return brought from thence is in canvass, oak, and spruce, plank and timber, sturgeon, some hemp and flax, pot ashes, &c., but chiefly corn.

Here the Dutch have an infinite advantage of us, which is never to be surmounted or overcome, and for which reason it is impossible for us ever to beat them out of this trade; viz., the Dutch send yearly a very great number of ships to Dantzic, &c., to fetch corn; some say they send a thousand sail every year; and I believe they do send so many ships, or those ships going so many times, or making so many voyages in the year as amounts to the same number of freights, and so is the same thing.

All these ships going for corn for the Dutch, have their chief supply of corn from that country; it follows, then, that their herrings are carried for nothing, seeing the ships which carry them must go light if they did not carry the fish; whereas, on the other hand, our fish must pay freight in whatever vessel it may go.

When our ships, then, from Scotland, for there the fishery chiefly lies, and from thence the trade must take its rise; I say, when they have carried their fish to the ports above-named, of Dantzic and Konigsberg, how must they come back, and with what shall they be loaded?

The only answer that can be given is, that they must bring back the goods mentioned before, or, in shorter terms, naval stores, though indeed not much of naval stores neither, except timber and plank, for the hemp and tar, which are the main articles, are fetched further; viz., from Riga, Revel, Narva, and Petersburg. But suppose after delivering their fish, some of the ships should go to those ports to seek freight, and load naval stores there, which is the utmost help in the trade that can be expected.

The next question is, whither shall they carry them, and for whose account shall they be loaden? To go for Scotland, would not be an answer; for Scotland, having but a few ships, could not take off any quantity proportioned to such a commerce; for if we were to push the Dutch out of the trade, we must be supposed to employ two or three hundred sail of ships at least, to carry herrings to Dantzic, &c.

To say they might take freight at London, and load for England, would be no answer neither; for besides that even England itself would not take off a quantity of those goods equal to the number of ships which would want freight, so if England did, yet those ships would still have one dead freight, for they would be left to go light home at last, to Scotland, otherwise how shall they be at hand to load next year? And even that one dead freight would abate the profit of the voyage; and so still the Dutch would have the advantage.

Upon the whole, take it how and which way we will, it will for ever be true, that though our fish were every way equal to the Dutch, which yet we cannot affirm, and though it came as soon to market, and carried as good a price there, all which I fear must a little fall short, yet it would still be true that the Dutch would gain and we should lose.

There is yet another addition to the advantage of Holland, viz., in the return of money; that whereas when our fish shall be sold, we shall want to remit back the produce in money; that is to say, so much of it as cannot be brought back in goods. And the difference in the exchange must be against us; but it is in favour of the Dutch; for if they did not send their herrings and other fish to Dantzic, they must remit money to pay for their corn; and even as it is, they are obliged to send other goods, such as whale oil, the produce of their Greenland fishery, English manufactures, and the like; whereas the Scots' merchants, having no market for corn, and not a demand for a sufficient value in naval stores, &c., viz. the product of the country, must bring the overplus by exchange to their loss, the exchange running the other way.

It is true, this is a digression; but it is needful to show how weak those notions are, which prompt us to believe we are able to beat the Dutch out of the fishing trade by increasing our number of busses, and taking a larger quantity of fish.

But this brings me back to the first argument; if you can find a way to enlarge your shipping in the fishery, and send greater quantities of fish to market, and yet sell them to advantage, you would by consequence enlarge your demand for naval stores, and so be able to bring more ships home loaden from thence; that is to say, to dispose of more of their freight at home; and indeed nothing else can do it.

N. B. This very difference in the trade is the reason why a greater quantity of English manufactures are not sent from hence to Dantzic, as was formerly done; viz., not that the consumption of those goods is lessened in Poland, or that less woollen manufactures are demanded at Dantzic or at Konigsberg; but it is that the Dutch carry our manufactures from their own country; this they can do to advantage; besides their costing nothing freight, as above, though they are sold to little or no profit, because they want the value there to pay for their corn, and must otherwise remit money to loss for the payment.

As these things are not touched at before in any discourses on this subject, but we are daily filled with clamours and complaints at the indolence and negligence of our Scots and northern Britons, for not outworking the Dutch in their fishing trade, I think it is not foreign to the purpose to have thus stated the case, and to have shown that it is not indeed a neglect in our management, that the Dutch thrive in the fishing trade, and we sit still, as they call it, and look on, which really is not so in fact, but that the nature of the thing gives the advantage to the Dutch, and throws the trade into their hands, in a manner that no industry or application of ours could or can prevent.

Having thus vindicated our people where they are really not deserving blame, let us look forward from hence and see with the same justice where they are in another case likewise less to blame than is generally imagined; namely, in the white fishing, or the taking of cod-fish in these northern seas, which is also represented as if it was so plentiful of fish that any quantity might be taken and cured, and so the French, the Scots, and the Portuguese, might be supplied from hence much cheaper and more to advantage than by going so long a voyage as to the banks of Newfoundland.

This also is a mistake, and the contrary is evident; that there is a good white fishing upon the coast, as well of the north part of the British coast as on the east side of Scotland, is very true; the Scots, to give them their due, do cure a tolerable quantity of fish, even in or near the frith of Edinburgh; also there is a good fishery for cod on the west side, and among the islands of the Leuze, and the other parts called the western islands of Scotland; but the mistake lies in the quantity, which is not sufficient to supply the demand in those ports mentioned above, nor is it such as makes it by far so easy to load a ship as at Newfoundland, where it is done in the one-fifth part of the time, and consequently so much cheaper; and the author of this has found this to be so by experience.

Yet it cannot be said with justice that the Scots' fishermen are negligent, and do not improve this fishing to advantage, for that really they do kill and cure as many as can be easily done to make them come within a price, and more cannot be done; that is to say, it would be to no purpose to do it; for it will for ever be true in trade, that what cannot be done to advantage, may be said not to be possible to be done; because gain is the end of commerce, and the merchant cannot do what he cannot get by.

It may be true that in the herring fishery the consumption might be increased at home, and in some places also abroad, and so far that fishery is not so fully pursued; but I do not see that the increase of it can be very considerable, there being already a prodigious quantity cured more than ever in Ireland on every side of that kingdom, and also on the west of England; but if it may be increased, so much the more will be the advantage of the commerce; of which by itself.

But from this I come to the main article of the British trade, I mean our wool, or, as it is generally expressed, the woollen manufacture, and this is what I mean, when I said as above, spin and live.

In this likewise I must take the liberty to say, and insist upon it, that the English people cannot be said to be idle or slothful, or to neglect the advantages which are put into their hands of the greatest manufactures in Europe, if not in the whole world.

On the other hand, the people of England have run up their manufactures to such a prodigy of magnitude, that though it is extended into almost every part of the known world, I mean, the world as it is known in trade; yet even that whole world is scarce equal to its consumption, and is hardly able to take off the quantity; the negligence therefore of the English people is not so much liable to reproof in this part, as some pretend to tell us; the trade of our woollen manufacture being evidently increased within these few years past, far beyond what it ever was before.

I know abundance of our people talk very dismal things of the decay of our woollen manufacture, and that it is declined much they insist upon it; being prohibited in many places and countries abroad, of their setting up other manufactures of their own in the room of it, of their pretending to mimick and imitate it, and supply themselves with the produce of their own land, and the labour of their own people, and indeed France has for many years gone some length in this method of erecting woollen manufactures in the room of ours, and making their own productions serve instead of our completely finished manufacture: but all these imitations are weak and unperforming, and show abundantly how little reason we have to apprehend their endeavours, or that they will be able to supplant our manufacture there or any where else; for that even in France itself, where the imitation of our manufactures is carried on to the utmost perfection; yet they are obliged to take off great quantities of our finest and best goods; and such is the necessity of their affairs, that they to this day run them in, that is, import them clandestinely at the greatest risk, in spite of the strictest prohibition, and of the severest penalties, death and the galleys excepted; a certain token that their imitation of our manufactures is so far from pleasing and supplying other parts of the world, that they are not sufficient to supply, or good enough to please themselves.

I must confess the imitating our manufactures has been carried further in France than in any other part of the world, and yet we do not see they have been able so to affect the consumption as to have any visible influence upon our trade; or, that we abate the quantity which we usually made, but that if they have checked the export at all, we have still found other channels of trade which have fully carried off our quantity, and shall still do so, though other nations were able to imitate us to, and this is very particularly stated and explained by the author of the book above mentioned, called the Plan of the English Commerce, where the extending our manufactures is handled more at large than I have room for in the narrow compass of this tract, and therefore I again refer my reader thither, as to the fountain head.

But I go on to touch the heads of things. The French do imitate our manufactures in a better manner, and in greater quantity than other nations; and why do we not prevent them? It is a terrible satire upon our vigilance, or upon the method of our custom-house men, that we do not prevent it; seeing the French themselves will not stick to acknowledge, that without a supply of our wool, which is evident they have now with very small difficulty from Ireland, they could do little in it, and indeed nothing at all to the purpose.

On the other hand, it is not so with France in regard to their silk manufactures, in which although we have not the principles of the work, I mean the silk growing within our dominions, but are obliged to bring it from Italy, yet we have so effectually shut out the French silk manufactures from our market, that in a word we have no occasion at all for them; nay, if you will believe some of our manufacturers, the French buy some of our wrought silks and carry them into France; but whether the particular be so in fact or no, this I can take upon me from good evidence to affirm, that whereas we usually imported in the ordinary course of trade, at least a million to twelve hundred thousand pounds' value a year in wrought silks from France; now we import so little as is not worth naming; and yet it is allowed that we do not wear less silk, or silks of a meaner value, than we usually did before, so that all the difference is clear gain on the English side in the balance of trade.

The contemplation of this very article furnishes a most eminent encouragement to our people, to increase and improve their trade; and especially to gain upon the rest of Europe, in making all the most useful manufactures of other nations their own.

Nor would this increase of our trade be a small article in the balance of business, when we come to calculate the improvement we have made in that particular article, by encroaching upon our neighbours, more than they have been able to make upon us; and this also you will find laid down at large in the account of the improvement of our manufactures in general, calculated in the piece above mentioned, chap. v. p. 164.

If then the encroachments of France upon our woollen manufactures are so small, as very little to influence our trade, or lessen the quantity made here, and would be less if due care was taken to keep our wool out of their hands; and that at the same time we have encroached upon their trade in the silk manufactures only, besides others, such as paper, glass, linen, hats, &c., to the value of twelve hundred thousand pounds a year, then France has got little by prohibiting the English manufactures, and perhaps had much better have let it alone.

However, I must not omit here what is so natural a consequence from these premises, viz., that here lies the first branch of our Humble Proposal to the People of England for Increase of their Commerce, and Improvement of their Manufactures; namely, that they would keep their wool at home.

I know it will be asked immediately how shall it be done? and the answer indeed requires more time and room to debate it, than can be allowed me here. But the general answer must be given; certainly it is practicable to be done, and I am sure it is absolutely necessary. I shall say more to it presently.

But I go on with the discourse of the woollen manufactures in general; nothing is more certain, than that it is the greatest and most extensive branch of our whole trade, and, as the piece above mentioned says positively, is really the greatest manufacture in the world. Vide Plan, chap. v. p. 172. 179.

Nor can the stop of its vent, in this or that part of the world, greatly affect it; if foreign trade abates its demand in one place, it increases it in another; and it certainly goes on increasing prodigiously every year, in direct confutation of the phlegmatic assertions of those, who, with as much malice as ignorance, endeavour to run it down, and depreciate its worth as well as credit, by their ill-grounded calculations.

We might call for evidence in this cause the vast increase of our exportation in the woollen manufactures only to Portugal; which, for above twenty-five years past, has risen from a very moderate trade to such a magnitude, that we now export more woollen goods in particular yearly to Portugal, than both Spain and Portugal took off before, notwithstanding Spain has been represented as so extraordinary a branch of trade. The occasion of this increase is fully explained, by the said Plan of the English Commerce, to be owing to the increase of the Portuguese colonies in the Brazils, and in the kingdoms of Congo and Angola on the west side of Africa; and of Melinda and the coast of Zanguebar on the east side; in all which the Portuguese have so civilized the natives and black inhabitants of the country, as to bring them, where they went even stark naked before, to clothe decently and modestly now, and to delight to do so, in such a degree as they will hardly ever be brought to go unclothed again; and all these nations are clothed more or less with our English woollen manufactures, and the same in proportion in their East India factories.

The like growth and increase of our own colonies, is another article to confirm this argument, viz., that the consumption of our manufactures is increased: it is evident that the number of our people, inhabitants of those colonies, visibly increases every day; so must by a natural consequence the consumption of the cloths they wear.

And this increase is so great, and is so demonstrably growing every day greater, that it is more than equal to all the decrease occasioned by the check or prohibitions put upon our manufactures, whether by the imitation of the French or any other European nation.

I might dwell upon this article, and extend the observation to the East Indies, where a remarkable difference is evident between the present and the past times; for whereas a few years past the quantity of European goods, whether of English or other manufactures, was very small, and indeed not worth naming; on the contrary, now the number of European inhabitants in the several factories of the English, Dutch, and Portuguese, is so much increased, and the people who are subject to them also, and who they bring in daily to clothe after the European fashion, especially at Batavia, at Fort St. George, at Surat, Goa, and other principal factories, that the demand for our manufactures is grown very considerable, and daily increasing. This also the said Plan of the Commerce insists much on, and explains in a more particular manner.

But to proceed: not only our English colonies and factories are increased, as also the Portuguese in the Brazils, and in the south part of Africa; not only the factories of the English and Dutch in the East Indies are increased, and the number of Europeans there being increased call for a greater quantity of European goods than ever; but even the Spaniards, and their colonies in the West Indies, I mean in New Spain, and other dominions of the Spaniards in America, are increased in people, and that not so much the Spaniards themselves, though they too are more numerous than ever, but the civilized free Indians, as they are called, are exceedingly multiplied.

These are Indians in blood, but being native subjects of Spain, know no other nation, nor do they speak any other language than Spanish, being born and educated among them. They are tradesmen, handicrafts, and bred to all kinds of business, and even merchants too, as the Spaniards are, and some of them exceeding rich; of these they tell us there are thirty thousand families in the city of Lima only, and doubtless the numbers of these increase daily.

As all these go clothed like Spaniards, as well themselves as their wives, children, and servants, of which they have likewise a great many, so it necessarily follows that they greatly increase the consumption of European goods, and that the demand of English manufactures in particular increases in proportion, these manufactures being more than two-thirds of the ordinary habit or dress of those people, as it is also of the furniture of their houses; all which they take from their first patrons, the Spaniards.

It will seem a very natural inquiry here, how I can pretend to charge the English nation with indolence or negligence in their labouring or working their woollen manufactures; when it is apparent they work up all the wool which their whole nation produces, that the whole growth and produce of their sheep is wrought up by them, and that they buy a prodigious quantity from Ireland and Scotland, and work up all that too, and that with this they make such an infinite quantity of goods, that they, as it were, glut and gorge the whole world with their manufactures.

My answer is positive and direct, viz., that notwithstanding all this, they are chargeable with an unaccountable, unjustifiable, and, I had almost said, a most scandalous indolence and neglect, and that in respect to this woollen manufacture in particular; a neglect so gross, that by it they suffer a manifest injury in trade. This neglect consists of three heads:

1. They do not work up all the wool which they might come at, and which they ought to work up, and about which they have still spare hands enough to set to work.

2. They with difficulty sell off or consume the quantity of goods they make; whereas they might otherwise vend a much greater quantity, both abroad and at home.

3. They do not sufficiently apply themselves to the improving and enlarging their colonies abroad, which, as they are already increased, and have increased the consumption of the manufactures, so they are capable of being much further improved, and would thereby still further improve and increase the manufactures. By so much as they do not work up the wool, by so much they neglect the advantage put into their hands; for the wool of Great Britain and Ireland is certainly a singular and exclusive gift from Heaven, for the advantage of this great and opulent nation. If Heaven has given the wool, and we do not improve the gift by manufacturing it all up, so far we are to be reproached with indolence and neglect; and no wonder if the wool goes from Ireland to France by whole shiploads at a time; for what must the poor Irish do with their wool? If they manufacture it we will not let them trade with those manufactures, or export them beyond sea. Our reasons for that prohibition are indeed very good, though too long to debate in this place: but no reason can be alleged that can in any sense of the thing be justifiable, why we should not either give leave to export the manufactures, or take the wool.

But to speak of the reason to ourselves, for the other is a reason to them (I mean the Irish). The reason to ourselves is this: we ought to take the wool ourselves, that the French might not have it to erect and imitate our own manufactures in France, and so supplant our trade.

Certainly, if we could take the whole quantity of the Irish wool off their hands, we might with ease prevent it being carried to France; for much of it goes that way, merely because they cannot get money for it at home.

This I charge therefore as a neglect, and an evident proof of indolence; namely, that we do not take effectual care to secure all the wool in Ireland; give the Irish money for it at a reasonable market price, and then cause it to be brought to England as to the general market.

I know it will be objected, that England does already take off as much as they can, and as much as they want; and to bring over more than they can use, will sink the market, and be an injury to ourselves; but I am prepared to answer this directly and effectually, and you shall have a full reply to it immediately.

But, in the mean time, this is a proof of the first proposition; namely, that we do not work up all our own wool, for the Irish wool is, and ought to be, esteemed as our own, in the present debate about trade; for that it is carried away from our own dominions, and is made use of by those that rival our manufactures to the ruin of our own trade.

That the Irish are prohibited exporting their wool, is true; but it seems a little severe to prohibit them exporting their wool, and their manufactures too, and then not to buy the wool of them neither.

It is alleged by some, that we do take off all the wool they bring us, and that we could and would take it all, if they would bring it all. To this I answer; if the Irish people do not bring it all to us, it is either that it is too far for the poor people who own the wool to bring it to the south and east coast of Ireland, there being no markets in the west and north-west parts of that island, where they could sell it; and the farmers and sheep-breeders are no merchants, nor have they carriage for so long a journey; but either the public ought to appoint proper places whether it shall be carried, and where they would receive money for it at a certain rate; or erect markets where those who deal in wool might come to buy, and where those who have it to sell would find buyers.

No doubt but the want of buyers is the reason why so much of the Irish wool is carried over to France; besides, if markets were appointed where the poor farmers could always find buyers at one price or another, there would be then no pretence for them to carry it away in the dark, and by stealth, to the sea side, as is now the case; and the justice of prohibitions and seizures would be more easily to be defended; indeed there would be no excuse for the running it off, nor would there want any excuse for seizing it, if they attempted to run it off.

But I am called upon to answer the objection mentioned above; namely, that the manufactures in England do indeed already take off a very great quantity of the Irish wool, as much as they have occasion for; nay, they condescend so far to the Irish, as to allow them to manufacture a great deal of that wool which they take off; that is to say, to spin it into yarn, of which yarn so great a quantity is brought into England yearly, as they assure us amounts to sixty thousand packs of wool; as may be seen by a fair calculation in the book above mentioned, called the Plan; in a word, that the English are not in a condition to take off any more. Now this is that which leads me directly to the question in hand; whether the English are able to take off any more of the Irish wool and yarn, or no. I do not affirm, that, as the trade in England is now carried on, they are able, perhaps they are not; but I insist, that if we were thoroughly resolved in England to take such wise measures as we ought to take, and as we are well able to do, for the improvement and increase of our manufactures, we might and should be able to take off, and work up the whole growth of the wool of Ireland; and this I shall presently demonstrate, as I think, past doubt.

But before I come to the scheme for the performance of this, give me leave to lay down some particulars of the advantage this would be to our country, and to our commerce, supposing the thing could be brought to pass; and then I shall show how easily it might be brought to pass.

1. By taking off this great quantity of wool and yarn, supposing one half of the quantity to be spun, many thousands of the poor people of Ireland who are now in a starving condition for want of employment, would be set immediately to work, and be put in a condition to get their bread; so that it would be a present advantage to the Irish themselves, and that far greater than it can be now, their wool which goes away to France being all carried off unwrought.

2. Due care being then taken to prevent any exportation of wool to France, as, I take it for granted, might be done with much more ease when the Irish had encouragement to sell their wool at home, we

should soon find a difference in the expense of wool, by the French being disabled from imitating our manufactures abroad, and the consumption of our own would naturally increase in proportion. First, they would not be able to thrust their manufactures into foreign markets as they now do, by which the sale of our manufactures must necessarily be abated; and, secondly, they would want supplies at home, and consequently our manufactures would be more called for, even in France itself, and that in spite of penalties and prohibitions.

Thus by our taking off the Irish wool, we should in time prevent its exportation to France; and by preventing its going to France, we should disable the French, and increase the consumption of our own manufactures in all the ports whither they now send them, and even in France itself.

I have met with some people who have made calculations of the quantity of wool which is sent annually from Ireland to France, and they have done it by calculating, first how many packs of wool the whole kingdom of Ireland may produce; and this they do again from the number of sheep which they say are fed in Ireland in the whole. How right this calculation may be I will not determine.

First, they tell us, there are fed in Ireland thirty millions of sheep, and as all these sheep are supposed be sheared once every year, they must produce exactly thirty millions of fleeces, allowing the fell wool in proportion to the number of sheep killed.

It is observable, by a very critical account of the wool produced annually in Romney marsh, in the county of Kent, and published in the said Plan of the English Commerce, that the fleeces of wool of those large sheep, generally weigh above four pounds and a half each. It is computed thus; first he tells us that Romney marsh contains 47,110 acres of land, that they feed 141,330 sheep, whose wool being shorn, makes up 2,523 packs of wool, the sum of which is, that every acre feeds three sheep, every sheep yields one fleece, and 56 fleeces make one pack of wool, all which comes out to 2,523 packs of wool, twenty-three fleeces over, every pack weighing two hundred and forty pounds of wool. Vide Plan, &c. p. 259.

I need not observe here, that the sheep in Ireland are not near so large as the sheep in Romney marsh, these last being generally the largest breed of sheep in England, except a few on the bank of the river Tees in the bishoprick of Durham. Now if these large sheep yield fleeces of four pounds and a half of wool, we may be supposed to allow the Irish sheep, take them one with another, to yield three pounds of wool to a fleece, or to a sheep, out of which must be deducted the fell wool, most of which is of a shorter growth, and therefore cannot be reckoned so much by at least a pound to a sheep. Begin then to account for the wool, and we may make some calculation from thence of the number of sheep.

1. If of the Romney marsh fleeces, weighing four pounds and a half each, fifty-six fleeces make one pack of wool; then seventy fleeces Irish wool, weighing three pounds each fleece, make a pack.

2. If we import from Ireland one hundred thousand packs of wool, as well in the fleece as in the yarn, then we import the wool of seven millions of sheep fed in Ireland every year.

Come we next to the gross quantity of wool; as the Irish make all their own manufactures, that is to say, all the woollen manufactures, needful for their own use, such as for wearing apparel, house furniture, &c., we cannot suppose but that they use much more than the quantity exported to England, besides that, it is too well known, that notwithstanding the prohibition of exportation, they do daily ship off great quantities of woollen goods, not only to the West Indies, but also to France, to Spain, and Italy;

and we have had frequent complaints of our merchants from Lisbon and Oporto, of the great quantity of Irish woollen manufactures that are brought thither, as well broadcloth as serges, druggets, duroys, frieze, long-ells, and all the other sorts of goods which are usually exported from England; add these clandestine exportations to the necessary clothing, furniture, and equipages, of that whole nation, in which are reckoned two millions and a half of people, and we cannot suppose they make use of less than two hundred thousand packs of wool yearly among themselves, which is the wool of fourteen millions of sheep more.

We must, then, allow all the rest of the wool to be run or smuggled, call it what you please, to France, which must be at least a hundred to a hundred and twenty thousand packs more: for it seems the Irish tell us that they feed thirty millions of sheep in the whole kingdom of Ireland.

If, then, they run over to France a hundred thousand packs of wool yearly, which I take to be the least, all this amounts to twenty-eight millions of fleeces together; the other two millions of fleeces may justly be deducted for the difference between the quantity of wool taken from the sheep that are killed, which we call fell wool, and the fleece wool shorn.

Upon the foot of this calculation, there are a hundred thousand packs of wool produced in Ireland every year, which we ought to take off, and which, for want of our taking it off, is carried away to France, where it is wholly employed to mimick our manufactures and abuse our trade; lessening thereby the demand of our own goods abroad, and even in France itself. This, therefore, is a just reproach to our nation, and they are certainly guilty of a great neglect in not taking off that wool, and more effectually preventing it being carried away to France.

It must be confessed, that unless we do find some way to take off this wool from the Irish, we cannot so reasonably blame them for selling it to the French, or to anybody else that will buy, for what else can they do with it, seeing you shut up all their ports against the manufacturers; at least you shut them up as far as you are able; and if you will neither let them manufacture it, for not letting them transport the manufacture when made is in effect forbidding to make them; I say, if you will neither let them manufacture their wool nor take it off their hands, what must they do with it?

But I come next to the grand objection; namely, that we cannot take it off, that we do take off as much as we can use, and a very great quantity it is too; that we are not able to take more, that is to say, we know not what to do with it if we take it; that we cannot manufacture it, or if we do, we cannot sell the goods; and so, according to the known rule in trade, that what cannot be done with profit or without loss, we may say of it that it cannot be done; so in the sense of trade, we cannot take their wool off, and if they must run it over to France, they must, we cannot help it.

This, I say, is a very great mistake; and I do affirm, that as we ought to take off the whole quantity of the Irish wool, so we may and are able to do it. That our manufacture is capable of being so increased, and the consumption of it increased also, as well at home as abroad; that it would in the ordinary course of trade call for all the wool of Ireland, if it were much more than it is, and employ it profitably; besides employing many thousands of poor people more than are now employed, and who indeed want employment.

Upon this foundation, and to bring this to be true, as I shall presently make appear, I must add, that a just reproach lies upon us for indolence, and an unaccountable neglect of our national interests, in not sufficiently exerting ourselves to improve our trade and increase our manufactures; which is the title, as it is the true design, of this whole work.

The affirming, as above, that we are able to increase our manufacture, and by that increase to take off more wool, may, perhaps, be thought an arrogance too great to be justified, and would be a begging the question in an egregious manner, if I were not in a condition to prove what I say; I shall therefore apply myself directly to evidence, and to put it out of doubt:—

By increasing our manufacture, I am content to be understood to mean the increasing the consumption, otherwise, to increase quantity only, would be to ruin the manufacturers, not improve the trade. This increasing the consumption is to be considered under two generals.

1. The consumption at home.

2. The exportation, or consumption abroad.

I begin with the last; namely, the consumption abroad. This is too wide a field to enter upon in particular here, I refer it to be treated at large by itself; but as far as it serves to prove what I have affirmed above, namely, that the consumption of our manufactures may be improved abroad, so far it is needful to speak of it here; I shall confine it to the English colonies and factories abroad.

It is evident, that by the increase of our colonies, the consumption of our manufactures has been exceedingly increased; not only experience proves it, but the nature of the thing makes it impossible to be otherwise; the island of St. Christopher, is a demonstration beyond all argument; that island is increased in its product and people, by the French giving it up to us at the treaty of Utrecht. Its product of sugar is almost equal to that of Barbadoes, and will in a very few years exceed it; the exports from hence to that island are increased in proportion; why then do we not increase our possessions, plant new colonies, and better people our old ones? Both might be done to infinite advantage, as might be made out, had we room for it, past contradiction.

We talk of, and expect a war with Spain; were the advantages which new settlements in the abandoned countries of America, as well the island as the continent considered, we should all wish for such a war, that the English might by their superiority at sea, get and maintain a firm footing, as well on the continent as the islands of America: there the Spainards, like the fable of the dog in the manger, neither improve it themselves, nor will admit others to improve; I mean in all the south continent of America, from Buenos Ayres to port St. Julien, a country fruitful, a climate healthful, able to maintain plentifully any numbers, even to millions of people, with an uninterrupted communication within the land, as far as to the golden mountain of the Andes or Cordilleras, where the Chilians, unsubdued by any European power, a docible, civilized people, but abhorring the Spaniards, would not fail to establish a commerce infinitely profitable, exchanging gold for all your English manufactures, to an inexpressible advantage.

Among the islands, why should not we, as well as the French, plant upon the fruitful countries of Cuba and Hispaniola, as rich and capable of raising sugars, cocoa, ginger, pimento, indigo, cotton, and all the other productions usual in that latitude, as either the Barbadoes or Jamaica.

Our factories, for they cannot yet be called colonies, on the coast of Africa, offer us the like advantages. Why are they not turned into populous and powerful colonies, as they might be? Why not encouraged from hence? And why is not their trade espoused and protected as our other colonies and factories? but left to be ravaged by the naked and contemptible negroes; plundered, and their trade ravished by the more unjust and more merciless interlopers, who, instead of thieves, for they are no better, would be called separate traders only, though they break in by violence and fraud upon the property of an established company, and rob them of their commerce, even under the protection of their own forts and castles, which these paid nothing towards the cost of.

Why does not England enlarge and encourage the commerce of the coast of Guinea? plant and fortify, and establish such possessions there as other nations, the Portuguese for example, in the opposite coast on the same latitude? Is it not all owing to the most unaccountable indolence and neglect? What hinders but that we might ere now have had strong towns and an inhabited district round them, and a hundred thousand Christians dwelling at large in that country, as the Portuguese have now at Melinda, in the same latitude, on the eastern coast?

And what hinders, but that same indolence and neglect, that they have not there growing at this time, the coffee of Mocha, as the Dutch have at Batavia; the tea of China, the cocoa of the Caraccas, the spices of the Moluccas, and all the other productions of the remotest Indies, which grow now in the same latitude, and which cost us so much treasure yearly to purchase, and which, as has been tried, would prosper here as well as in the countries from which we fetch them?

What a consumption of English manufacture would follow such a plantation? and what an increase of trade would necessarily attend an increase of people there?

I have not room to enlarge here upon these heads; they are fully stated in the said Plan of English Commerce, and in several other tracts of trade lately published by the same author, and to that I refer. See the Plan, chap. iii. page 335. and chap. v. page 363.

I come next to the consumption at home, and here indeed the proof lies heavy upon ourselves; nothing but an unaccountable supreme negligence of our own apparent advantages can be the cause of the whole grievance; such a negligence, as I think, no nation but the English are, or can be guilty of; I mean no nation that has the like advantage of a manufacture, and that has a hundred thousand packs of wool every year unwrought up, and a million of people unemployed.

N. B. All our manufactures, whether of wool, silk, or thread, and all other wares, hard or soft, though we have a very great variety, yet do not employ all our people, by a great many; nay, we have some whole counties into which the woollen, or silk, or linen manufacture, may be said never to have set their feet, I mean as to the working part; or so little as not to be worth naming; such in particular as Cambridge, Huntingdon, Hertford, Bedford; the first three are of late indeed come into the spinning part a little, but it is but very little; the like may be said of the counties of Cheshire, Stafford, Derby, and Lincoln, in all which very little, if any, manufactures are carried on; neither are the counties of Kent, Sussex, Surry, or Hampshire, employed in any of the woollen manufactures worth mentioning; the last indeed on the side about Alton and Alresford, may be said to do a little; and the first just at Canterbury and Cranbrook. But what is all they do compared to the extent of four counties so populous that it is thought there are near a million of people in them?

Seeing then, I say, there are yet so many people want employ, and so much wool unwrought up, and which for want of being thus wrought up, is carried away by a clandestine, smuggling, pernicious trade, to employ our enemies in trade, the French, and to endanger our manufactures at foreign markets, how great is our negligence, and how much to the reproach of our country is it, that we do not improve this trade, and increase the consumption of the manufactures as we ought to do? I mean the consumption at home, for of the foreign consumption I have spoken already.

It seems to follow here as a natural inquiry, after what has been said, that we should ask, How is this to be done, and by what method can the people of England increase the home consumption of their woollen manufactures?

I cannot give a more direct answer to this question, or introduce what follows in a better manner, than in the very words of the author of the book so often mentioned above, as follows, speaking of this very thing, thus:—

"The next branch of complaint," says this author, "is, that the consumption of our woollen manufacture is lessened at home.

"This, indeed," continues he, "though least regarded, has the most truth and reason in it, and merits to be more particularly inquired into; but supposing the fact to be true, let me ask the complainer this question, viz., why do we not mend it? and that without laws, without teazing the parliament and our sovereign, for what they find difficult enough to effect even by law? The remedy is our own, and in our own power. I say, why do not the people of Great Britain, by general custom and by universal consent, increase the consumption of their own manufacture by rejecting the trifles and toys of foreigners?

"Why do we not appear dressed in the growth of our own country, and made fine by the labour of our own hands?" Vide Plan of the English Commerce, p. 252.

And again, p. 254; "We must turn the complaints of the people upon themselves, and entreat them to encourage the manufactures of England by a more general use and wearing of them. This alone would increase the consumption, as that alone would increase the manufacture itself."

I cannot put this into a plainer or better way of arguing, or in words more intelligible to every capacity.

Did ever any nation but ours complain of the declining of their trade and at the same time discourage it among themselves? Complain that foreigners prohibit our manufactures, and at the same time prohibit it themselves? for refusing to wear it is the worst and severest way of prohibiting it.

We do indeed put a prohibition upon our trade when we stop up the stream, and dam up the channel of its consumption, by putting a slight upon the wearing it, and, as it were, voting it out of fashion; for if you once vote your goods out of wear, you vote them out of the market, and you had as good vote them contraband.

With what an impetuous gust of the fancy did we run into the product of the East Indies for some years ago? How did we patiently look on and see the looms empty, the workmen fled, the wives and children starve and beg, the parishes loaded, and the poor's rates rise to a surprising height, while the ladies flourished in fine Massulapatam, chints, Indian damasks, China atlasses, and an innumerable number of rich silks, the product of the coast of Malabar, Coromandel, and the Bay of Bengal, and the poorer sort with calicoes? And with what infinite difficulty was a remedy obtained, and with what regret did the ladies part with that foreign pageantry, and stoop to wear the richest silks of their own manufacture, though these were the life of their country's prosperity, and those the ruin of it?

When this was the case, how fared our trade? The state of it was thus, in a few words:—

The poor, as above, wanted bread; the wool lay on hand, sunk in price, and wanted a market; the manufacturers wanted orders, and when they made goods, knew not where to sell them; all was melancholy and dismal on that side; nothing but the East India trade could be said to thrive; their ships went out full of money and came home full of poison; for it was all poison to our trade. The immense sums of ready money that went abroad to India impoverished our trade, and indeed bid fair to starve it, and, in a word, to beggar the nation.

At home we were so far from working up the whole quantity or growth of our wool, that three or four years' growth lay on hand in the poor tenants' houses, for want of which they could not pay their rent.

The wool from Scotland, which comes all to us now, went another way, viz., to France, for the Union was not then made, and yet we had too much at home. Nor was the quantity brought from Ireland half so much as it is now.

Was all this difference from our own wearing, or not wearing the produce of our own manufacture? How unaccountably stupid then are we to run still retrograde to the public good of our country, and ruin our own commerce, by rejecting our own manufacture, setting our people to furnish other nations with cloths, and recommending the manufacture to other countries, and rejecting them ourselves?

If the difference was small, and the clothing of our own people was a thing of small moment, that it made no impression on the commerce, or the manufacture in general, it might be said to be too little to take notice of.

If our consumption at home is thus considerable, and the clothing of our own people does consume the wool of many millions of sheep; if the silk trade employs many thousands of families; if there is an absolute necessity of working up if possible all the growth of our wool, as well of Ireland as of England, or that else it would be run over to France, to the encouragement of rival manufactures, and the ruin of our own; in a word, if our own people, falling into a general use of our own manufacture, would effectually do this, and their continuing to neglect it would effectually throw our manufacture into convulsions, and stagnate the whole trade of the kingdom; if our wearing foreign silk manufactures did annually carry out £1,200,000 sterling per annum for silks, to France and Italy, and above £600,000 per annum for the like to India, all in spices, to the impoverishing our trade, by emptying us of all our ready money, as well as starving our poor for want of employment.

Again, if these grievances were very much abated, and indeed almost remedied by the several acts of parliament, first to prohibit East India silks, then to lay high duties, equal to prohibition, upon French silks; and, in the last place, an act to prohibit the use and wearing of printed calicoes; I say, if these acts have gone so far in the retrieving the dying condition of our woollen manufacture, and encouraging the silk manufacture; that in the first, we have wrought up all the English growth of wool, and that of Scotland too, which was never done before; and in the last have improved so remarkably in the silk manufacture, that all that vast sum of £1,800,000 per annum, expended before in French and Indian silks, is now turned into the pockets of our own poor, and kept all at home, and the silks become a mere English manufacture as was before a foreign.

If all this is true, as it is most certainly, what witchcraft must it be that has seized upon the fancy of this nation? What spirit of blindness and infatuation must have possessed us? that we are in all haste running back into the old, stupid, and dull unthinking state, and growing fond of anything, nay of everything that is injurious to our own commerce, and be it as ruinous as it will to our own poor, and to our own manufactures; nay, though we see our trade sick and languishing, and our poor starving before our eyes; and know that we ourselves are the only cause of it, are yet so obstinately and unalterable averse to our own manufacture, and fond of novelties and trifles, that we will not wear our own goods, but will at any hazard make use of things foreign to us, the labour and advantage of strangers, pagans, negroes, or any kind of people, rather than our own.

Unhappy temper, unknown in any nation but ours! The wiser pagans and Mahometans, natives of India, Persia, China, Japan, Siam, Pegu, act otherwise; wherever we find any people in these parts, we find them clothed with their own manufacture, whether of silk, cotton, herba, or of whatever other materials they were made; nor to this day have our nicest or finest manufactures, though perfectly new to them, (and novelties we see take with us to a frenzy and distraction) touched their fancies, or so much as tempted them to wear them; all our endeavours to persuade them have been in vain; but with us, any new fancy, any far-fetched novelty, however antick, however extravagant in price, nay the dearer the more prevailing, presently touches our wandering fancy, and makes us cast off our finest and most agreeable produce, the fruit of our own industry, and the labour of our own poor, making a mode of the foreign gewgaw, let it be as wild and barbarous as it will.

But I meet with an objection in my way here, which is insisted upon with the utmost warmth; namely:—

Objection: you seem to acknowledge that the prohibition of India silks and the duties upon French silks, have effectually answered the end as to silks; and that the late act against the use and wearing of printed or painted calicoes has likewise had its effect on the woollen manufacture. There is nothing now left to support your complaint but the printed linen; which, though it is become a general wear, yet is our own product and growth, and the labour of our own poor; for the Scots and Irish, by whom the linen is manufactured, are our own subjects, and ought as much to be in our concern as any of the rest, and that linen is as much our own manufacture as the silk and the wool.

Nothing could, in my opinion, be more surprising of its kind, than to hear with what warmth this very argument was urged to the parliament, and to the public, by not the Scots and Irish only, but even by some of our own people, possessed and persuaded by the other, at the time the act against the printed calicoes was depending before the parliament; as if an upstart, and in itself trifling manufacture, however increased by the corruption of our people's humour and fancy, could be an equivalent to the grand manufacture of wool in England, which is the fund of our whole commerce, and has been the spring and fountain of our wealth and prosperity for above three hundred years; a manufacture which employs millions of our people, which has raised the wealth of the whole nation from what it then was to what it now is; a manufacture that has made us the greatest trading nation in the world, and upon which all our wealth and commerce still depends.

I insist upon it that no novelty is to be encouraged among us to the prejudice of this chief and main support of our country, let it be of what kind it will; nor is it at all to the purpose to say such or such a novelty is made at home, and is the work of our own people; it is to say nothing at all, for we ought no more to set up particular manufactures to the prejudice of the woollen trade in general, which is the grand product of the whole nation, and on which our whole prosperity depends, than we would spread an universal infection among us, on pretence that the vegetable or plant from whence the destructive effluvia proceeded, was the growth of our own land; or than we should publish the Alcoran and the most heretical, blasphemous, or immodest books, to taint the morals and principles of the people, on pretence that the paper and print were our own manufactures.

I am for encouraging all manufactures that can be invented and set up among us, and that may tend to the employment of the poor and improvement of our produce; such things having a national tendency to raising the rent of our lands, assisting the consumption of our growth, and, in a word, increasing trade in general; I say I am for encouraging new manufactures of all sorts, with this one exception only, namely, that they do not interfere with, and tend to the prejudice of the woollen manufacture, which is the main and essential manufacture of England.

But the woollen manufacture is the life and blood of the whole nation, the soul of our trade, the top of all manufactures, and nothing can be erected that either rivals it or any way lessens it or interferes with it, without wounding us in the more noble and vital part, and, in effect, endangering the whole.

To set up a manufacture of painted linen, which, touching the particular pride and gay humour of the ordinary sort of people, intercepts the woollen manufacture, which they would otherwise be clothed with, is so far wounding and supplanting the woollen manufacture for a paltry trifle, and though it is indeed in itself but a trifle, yet as the poorer sort of people, the servants, and the wives and children of the farmers and country people, and of the labouring poor, who wear this new fangle, are a vast multitude, the wound strikes deeper into the quantity than most people imagine, makes a large abatement of the consumption of wool, lessening the labour of the poor manufacturers very considerably; and on this account, I say, it ought not to be encouraged, though it be our own manufacture.

Do we not, from this very principle, prohibit the planting tobacco in England, though our own land would produce it? Do we not know there are coals in Blackheath, Muzzle-hill, and other places, but that we must not work them that we may not hurt the navigation? The reason is exactly the same here.

This consideration is so pungent in itself, and so naturally touches every Englishman that has the good of his country at heart, that one would think there should be no occasion for an act of parliament to oblige them to it; but they should be moved by a mere concern of mind, and generous endeavour for the public prosperity, not to fall in with or encourage any new project, any new custom or fashion, without first inquiring particularly whether it would not be injurious to the prosperity of the main and grand article of the English Commerce, the woollen manufacture.

Were this public spirit among us, we need fear no upstart manufacture breaking in upon us, whether printed linen or anything else; for no people of sense, having the good of their country at heart, would touch it, much less make it a general fashion. But, as the Plan of English Commerce observes, our people, the ladies especially, have such a passion for the fashion, that they have been the greatest enemies to our woollen manufacture; and I must add that this passion for the fashion of printed linens at this time is a greater blow to the woollen manufacture of England than all the prohibitions in Germany and Italy, of which we may have formed such frightful ideas in our minds; or even than all the imitation of our manufactures abroad, whether in France, or any other part of Europe.

And yet, to conclude all,

How easy, how very easy is it for us to prevent it; which, by the way, deserves a whole book by itself.

SECOND THOUGHTS ARE BEST: OR A FURTHER IMPROVEMENT OF A LATE SCHEME TO PREVENT STREET ROBBERIES: BY WHICH OUR STREETS WILL BE STRONGLY GUARDED, AND SO GLORIOUSLY ILLUMINATED, THAT ANY PART OF LONDON WILL BE AS SAFE AND PLEASANT AT MIDNIGHT AS AT NOONDAY; AND BURGLARY TOTALLY IMPRACTICABLE:

With Some Thoughts for suppressing Robberies in all the Public Roads of England, &c.

Humbly

Offered for the Good of his Country, submitted to the Consideration of the Parliament, and dedicated to his sacred Majesty King GEORGE II.

TO THE KING'S MOST EXCELLENT MAJESTY, SACRED AND MOST AUGUST!

Permit a loyal subject, in the sincerity of his heart, to press through the crowds of courtiers who surround your royal person, and lay his little mite, humbly offered for the public welfare, at your majesty's feet.

Happy is it for me, as well as the whole kingdom, we have a king of such humanity and affability; a king naturalized to us, a king who loves us, a king in whose person as well as mind, the whole hero appears: the king of our hearts; the king of our wishes!

Those who are dissatisfied with such a monarch, deserve to be abandoned of God, and have the devil sent to reign over them. Yet such there are, (pity they should wear human forms, or breathe the free air of Britain!) who are so scandalously fickle, that if God himself was to reign, they would yearn after their darling monarch the prince of darkness.

These are they who fly in the face of majesty, who so abuse the liberty of the press, that from a benefit it becomes an evil, and demands immediate regulation.

Not against your majesty only, but against many of your loyal subjects, are arrows shot in the dark, by lurking villains who wound the reputations of the innocent in sport. Our public newspapers, which ought to contain nothing but what is instructive and communicative, being now become public nuisances, vehicles of personal, private slander, and scandalous pasquins.

Let the glory be yours, most gracious sovereign! to suppress this growing evil; and if any hints from your most faithful subject can be of the least use, I live but to serve, to admire, and pray for your majesty.

Who am,
Most gracious Sovereign,
Your Majesty's Most loyal, most dutiful, most obedient subject and servant,

ANDREW MORETON.

Nothing is more easy than to discover a thing already found out. This is verified in me and that anonymous gentleman, whom the public prints have lately complimented with a Discovery to Prevent Street Robberies; though, by the by, we have only his vain ipse dixit, and the ostentatious outcry of venal newswriters in his behalf.

But to strip him of his borrowed plumes, these are to remind the public, that about six months ago, in a treatise, entituled, Augusta Triumphans: or, the Way to make London the most flourishing City in the Universe, I laid down a plain and practicable scheme for the total suppression and prevention of street robberies, which scheme has been approved of by several learned and judicious persons.

Oh! but say the advocates of this second-hand schemist, our project is to be laid before the parliament. Does that make his better, or mine worse? Have not many silly projects been laid before parliaments ere now? Admit it be not the same (as I have but too much reason to fear it is,) cannot the members of both houses read print as well as written hand? Or does he think they are so prejudiced to dislike a thing the worse for being offered without view of gain? I trust Andrew Moreton's scheme, generously offered for the public good, will meet with as fair a reception as that of this hireling projector.

Mine is already published; let him generously follow my example, and no doubt, if his scheme be preferred, the government will reward him.

If my antagonist be necessitous, where is the merit? he does it for his own sake, not for the public. If he be not necessitous, what a sordid wretch is he to withhold his scheme for lucre? putting it up at public sale; so that if you do not give him his price you shall not have it.

Some people, indeed, are so fond of mysteries they run down everything that is plain and intelligible; they love darkness, whispers, and freemasonry, despising whatever comes in the shape of a pamphlet, be it never so useful or commendable. But in spite of prejudice, truth is the standard by which I hope all honest and impartial men will judge me.

Though I must confess I am not a little piqued to be jockeyed out of my labours, yet not to be behindhand with my gentleman in the clouds, who would have the parliament buy his pig in a poke, and build up his fortune at my expense, I have so amply enlarged and amended my scheme, that it is now scarce like the same. I have taken in everything possible of comprehension or practice; nor have I left him room to edge in one single hint. I have debated the objections of divers wise and learned men, and corrected my project accordingly; so that, on comparison, my first thoughts will appear but as a rude and imperfect sketch, only valuable in that it gave the idea of this more laboured and finished performance, on which I pledge my whole reputation, being ready to stand or fall by its success.

In order to which, I have presented copies of this book to the king and queen's most excellent majesties, to several of the lords spiritual, and divers honourable and worthy members of both houses, and time must show whose scheme shall have the precedence.

In the mean time I stand prepared for the sneers of those who despise everything and everybody but their own dear selves, as also the objections of the puzzle causes, who will turry-lugg a thing out of all sense and meaning, and by the cloudiness of their explanations darken what is most plain and obvious. My business is to go straight forward, and let the end crown the work. If men of sense approve me, I need not value the laughter of fools, whose very approbation is scandal; for if a thinking man is to be laughed out of every good intention or invention, nothing will ever be done for the public good.

SECOND THOUGHTS, &c.

The principal encouragement and opportunity given to our street robbers is, that our streets are so poorly watched; the watchmen, for the most part, being decrepit, superannuated wretches, with one foot in the grave and the other ready to follow; so feeble that a puff of breath can blow them down. Poor crazy mortals! much fitter for an almshouse than a watchhouse. A city watched and guarded by such animals is wretchedly watched indeed.

Nay, so little terror do they carry with them, that hardy thieves make a mere jest of them, and oftentimes oblige even the very watchman who should apprehend, to light them in their roguery. And what can a poor creature do, in terror of his life, surrounded by a pack of ruffians, and no assistance near?

Add to this, that our rogues are grown more wicked than ever, and vice in all kinds is so much winked at, that robbery is accounted a petty crime. We take pains to puff them up in their villany, and thieves are set out in so amiable a light in the Beggar's Opera, it has taught them to value themselves on their profession rather than to be ashamed of it.

There was some cessation of street robberies, from the time of Bunworth and Blewitt's execution, until the introduction of this pious opera. Now we find the Cartouchian villanies revived, and London, that used to be the most safe and peaceful city in the universe, is now become a scene of rapine and danger. If some of Cartouch's gang be not come over hither to instruct our thieves, we have, doubtless, a Cartouch of our own, and a gang which, if not suppressed, may be full as pernicious as was ever Cartouch's, and London may be as dangerous as Paris, if due care be not taken.

Not content with the mischief done by the Beggar's Opera, we must have a Quaker's Opera, forsooth, of much more evil tendency than the former; for in this Jack Shepherd is made the hero of the drama, and runs through such a scene of riot and success, that but too many weak minds have been drawn away, and many unwary persons so charmed with his appearance on the stage, dressed in that elegant manner, and his pockets so well lined, they have forthwith commenced street-robbers or housebreakers; so that every idle fellow, weary of honest labour, need but fancy himself a Macheath or a Shepherd, and there is a rogue made at once. Since, therefore, example, has such force, the stage ought to be reformed, and nothing exhibited but what might be represented before a bishop. They may be merry and wise: let them take the Provoked Husband for a pattern.

A good physician seeks the cause, and weighs the symptoms before he proceeds to prescribe; and if we trace this evil from its radix, we shall find a cause antecedent to the two operas aforesaid: namely, accursed Geneva, the bane and ruin of our lower class of people.

Those who deny an inferior class of people to be necessary in a body politic, contradict reason and experience itself; since they are most useful when industrious, and equally pernicious when lazy. By their industry our manufactures, trade, and commerce, are carried on. The merchant in his counting-house, and the captain in his cabin, would find but little employment, were it not that many hands carried on the different branches of the concerns they superintended.

But now so far are our common people infatuated with Geneva, that half the work is not done now as formerly. It debilitates and enervates them, nor are they near so strong and healthy as formerly.

So that if this abuse of Geneva be not stopped, we may go whoop for husbandmen, labourers, &c.; trade must consequently stand still, and the credit of the nation sink. Nor is the abatement of the excise, though very considerable, and most worthy notice, any ways comparable to the corruption of manners, destruction of health, and all the train of evils we are threatened with from pernicious Geneva.

We will suppose a man able to maintain himself and family by his trade, and at the same time to be a Geneva drinker. This fellow first makes himself incapable of working by being continually drunk; which runs him behindhand, so that he either pawns, or neglects his work, for which reason nobody will employ him. At last, fear of arrests, his own hunger, the cries of a family for bread, his natural desire to support an irregular life, and a propense hatred to labour, turn but too many an honest tradesman into an arrant desperate rogue. And these are commonly the means that furnish us with thieves and villains in general.

Thus is a man, who might be useful in a body politic, rendered obnoxious to the same: so that if this trade of wickedness goes on, they will increase upon us so much that we shall not dare to stir out of our habitations; nay, it will be well if they arrive not to the impudence of plundering our houses at noonday.

Where is the courage of the English nation, that a gentleman, with six or seven servants, shall be robbed by one single highwayman? Yet we have lately had instances of this; and for this we may thank our effeminacy, our toupee wigs, and powdered pates, our tea, and other scandalous fopperies; and, above all, the disuse of noble and manly sports, so necessary to a brave people, once in vogue, but now totally lost amongst us.

Let not the reader think I run from my subject if I search the bottom of the distemper before I propose a cure, which having done, though indeed but slightly, for this is an argument could be carried to a much greater length, I proceed to the purpose in manner following:—

Let the watch be composed of stout able-bodied men, and of those a sufficient number, that is to say, a watchman to every forty houses, twenty on one side of the way, and twenty on the other; for it is observable that a man cannot well see distinctly beyond the extent of twenty houses in a row; if it is a single row, and no opposite houses, the charge must be greater, or their safety less.

This man should be elected and paid by the housekeepers themselves, to prevent misapplication and abuse, so much complained of in the distribution of the public money.

He should be allowed ten shillings per annum by each housekeeper, which at forty houses, as above specified, amounts to 20l. per annum, almost treble to what is at present allowed; and yet most housekeepers are charged at least 2s. 6d. a quarter to the watch, whose beat is, generally speaking, little less than the compass of half a mile.

What a shame it is that at least £100 should be collected in some beats, and the poor watchman should not have the one-tenth part of the money? And this I leave to the consideration of any housekeeper who will take the pains to inquire into the extent of a watchman's beat, and after that cast up what is collected in the said beat, as they say for the watch. But this is a small abuse in comparison of other parochial misapplications, for a proof of which I refer my reader to a treatise of mine, entituled, Parochial Tyranny.

This salary of £20 per annum is something of encouragement, and a pretty settlement for a poor man, who with frugality may live decently thereon, and by due rest be enabled to give due and vigilant attendance; that is to say, from evening dusk to morning light.

If a housekeeper break, or a house is empty, the poor watchman ought not to suffer, the deficiency should be made up by the housekeepers remaining.

The watch thus stationed, strengthened, and encouraged, let every watchman be armed with firearms and sword; and let no watchman stand above twenty doors distant from his fellow.

This has already been put in practice in the parish of St. Giles's in the Fields, and has had so good an effect that it is hoped other parishes will follow their example, which redounds not a little to the credit of our project.

Let each watchman be provided with a horn, to sound an alarm, or in time of danger; and let it be made penal, if not felony, for any but a watchman to sound a horn in and about the city, from the time of their going on, to that of their going off.

I know an objection will be here made on account of the postboys, to obviate which, I had thoughts of a bell, but that would be too ponderous and troublesome for a watchman to carry, besides his arms and lantern; whereas a horn is portable, always ready, and most alarming.

Let the postboys therefore use some other signal, since this is most convenient to this more material purpose. They may carry a bell in a holster with ease, and give notice by that, as well as those who collect the letters.

That the watchmen may see from one end of their walks to the other, let a convenient number of lamps be set up, and those not of the convex kind, which blind the eyes, and are of no manner of use; they dazzle, but give no distinct light, and further, rather than prevent robberies. Many persons, deceived and blinded by these ignes fatui, have been run over by coaches, carts, &c., people stumbling more, even under these very lamps, than in the dark. In short, they are most unprofitable lights, and, in my opinion, rather abuses than benefits.

Besides, I see no reason why every ten housekeepers cannot find a lamp among themselves, which would be four lamps in a beat, and let their watchman dress it, rather than fatten a crew of directors.

But we are so fond of companies, it is a wonder we have not our shoes blacked by one, and a set of directors made rich at the expense of our very black-guards.

The watch ought to be in view, as well as in the hearing of each other, or they may be overpowered, and much danger may happen.

The streets being thus gloriously illuminated, and so strongly guarded by stout and able fellows, well armed and well paid, all within the view of one another, proceed we to secure all by-turnings, courts, alleys, lanes, &c., which may favour a street-robber's escape, and make our project ineffectual.

A street, court, lane, alley, or other place, where the number of houses or poverty of the inhabitants will not afford a watchman on the terms before mentioned, should be gated in, and the inhabitants let in and out by the watchman of the street.

Where there are even but twelve houses in a court, and the inhabitants people of credit, they may have a separate watch to themselves, as is practised in Boswell-court by Lincoln's-inn-fields, Angel-court in Throckmorton-street, and many other places in London.

This I think an unexceptionable way to secure the cities and suburbs of London and Westminster. The only difficulty I can conceive is, that persons after dark may now and then go a little way round about by keeping the street way, but the pleasantness and safety occasioned by the lights and watch aforesaid, make ample amends. Let those go through byways, and in the dark, whose deeds are so; I am for providing security for honest men, and obstacle for rogues.

And now we have put a stop to their roguery, let us endeavour to suppress the rogues themselves; in order to which I shall begin with their harlots, who are, generally speaking, the first motives to their villany, and egg them on to all manner of mischief.

And these are generally servant wenches, who stroll from place to place, and at last, weary of working, throw themselves on the public. To maintain these creatures, many a man turns rogue. It behoves the government, therefore, to oblige all young wenches to keep in service. Masters and mistresses ought likewise to see that servants of both sexes go not a rambling when sent to church, but that they keep good hours; for many have been ruined by junketing and staying out, instead of being at church or at home.

Our common women ought to be restrained in the liberties they have lately taken; they openly swear and talk so obscenely, it is a shame to a Christian country.

Having fully handled this topic in two treatises, viz., Everybody's Business is Nobody's Business, and Parochial Tyranny, I shall not tire my readers with repetition, but referring them to the treatises themselves, return to my subject, which is,—

After we have reformed the ladies, let us take their sparks in hand. And first, let all shoe-cleaners, I mean boys and sturdy vagrants, be suppressed, according to my scheme in Everybody's Business, &c.; as for link-boys, alias thieves with lights, there will be no need of them when the streets are illuminated, according to my project.

That sailors as well as soldiers may not give cause of suspicion, it is fit they should also be quartered after the same nature; and more to enforce it, surveyors of quarters should have rounds allotted them.

These surveyors should call at the quarters of every soldier or sailor at a limited hour, to see if they are there or no, and register them at home or absent accordingly; absence to be penal.

Every soldier or sailor leaving his quarters till morning, after he has been found at home and registered, should be punished.

I must be excused if I ward every obstacle, my design being to break up street-robbers, nest and egg.

And that thieves may not stroll about, under pretence of being destitute of lodging, barracks or barns should be built at convenient ends of the town, where all vagrants should be obliged to render themselves at a stated hour, where they should have clean straw allowed them, and be kept orderly and out of harm's way; they may be let loose if they have apparent means of honest livelihood, otherwise they should be sent to the workhouse of their respective parish, or to a general workhouse, of which there is great need; and of which more hereafter.

All publichouses and gin-shops, if they should be tolerated, should be shut up at ten.

If the government should think fit to tolerate gin-shops, I see no reason why they may not be subject to licenses, and come into the pot-act as well as alehouses; especially considering there is as much gin as ale consumed nowadays.

Night houses and cellars, above all, should be totally suppressed; these are the harbours and refuge of villains and strumpets; these are their houses of call where there hellish trade is carried on; it is here they wait for the signal of their scouts; here they cast their schemes, and bring in advices; here they encourage and initiate young thieves; here they barter and sell their stolen goods; these are their exchanges and asylums after mischief.

Hackney coach drivers next require our care; they are the scum of the people, and, generally speaking, the worst of rogues.

So many and such frequent robberies can never be committed without the connivance of these villains; and it is but too much to be feared, that at the same time they take up a fare they take up a robber, who is ready to mark his prey, and gets up either on the box or behind; and alights at a convenient place to perpetrate his hellish design. As for a 'snack of the coal' as they term it, no doubt but the coachman and he have proper understanding and rendezvous.

Many who go to the coach-office nowadays, may be mistaken in their hopes of redress, not but the commissioners to a man treat complainants with the utmost civility; but the penalty, which used to be on the renter, being now on the driver, the renter or owner of that figure is clear, and the driver has nothing to do but to be absent and laugh at the complainant, an instance of which take in the following case:—

A hackney coachman took eighteenpence of a gentleman for a twelvepenny fare; the gentleman took his number and complained; the driver appeared, and was fined fifteen shillings, but the renter escaped; what was the result? The driver absconded, the gentleman sits down at his loss of attendance and money; had robbery or assault been the complaint, the consequence had been the same, the gentleman is but where he was. He has since called several times at the office, but to no purpose; all the answer he can get is, the fellow cannot be found. I write this therefore to undeceive those persons, who think when they have taken the number of a coach they can punish the driver for insolence or extortion.

The law in this case ought to be turned into its old channel, that is to say, the owner of the figure should be answerable; he ought to employ a driver he can answer for, or drive himself.

Every renter therefore should be obliged to register, and respond for his driver; or commissioners, figures, and all other forms, are to little purpose.

Beggars should next be suppressed, who lounge about all day, to see where they can steal at night. It is a shame we should suffer real objects of charity to beg; and for those who are not so, it is a shame but they should work.

I shall close all with these observations:—

That the extortions and cabals of tradesmen, by enhancing the prices of provisions, is most detrimental to a state, and worthy the notice of its legislature; for men not being able to support their families by honest labour, and being made beggars by reason of the dearness of provisions, ofttimes grow desperate and turn rogues. This assertion is but too true, to prove which I appeal to the late conduct of

The coal merchants,
The bakers,
The butchers,
And, above all, the tallow chandlers.

The cabals of coal traders have for many years jockeyed us in the price of coals; they have raised and fell them at pleasure, and made mere stockjobbing work of it; but never so much as in his late majesty's reign; on a great impress for seamen, they, in less than a fortnight, raised the price of coals from twenty-three shillings to almost fifty. What a pinch must this be on the poor, who live only from hand to mouth, and buy their coals, poor souls! some by the half peck.

The bakers are yet more flagrant and vile; they turn plenty to famine, and push up the price of bread without rule or reason; they have already been detected in one bite, i.e., procuring some of the fraternity to buy a small quantity of corn much above the market price, and then, by making oath thereof, abuse a well-intended law, and raise the price of bread accordingly.

Thus are the poor ground to dust, in order to fatten a pack of misers, who know no mercy. But I hope the government will make them honest, even against their will.

The butchers are now so extravagant in their way of living, that usual and moderate profit will not content them; they cannot drink malt liquor, and the poor must pay for the wine, which they swill down at an unmerciful rate.

The price of meat should therefore be regulated according to the price of cattle, but not according to the baker's rule afore mentioned.

But as for the tallow-chandlers, their oppressions call aloud for redress. To what an exorbitant pitch have they raised candles; just double what it was some years ago: nay, they threaten to have them at tenpence per pound. How can the poor work when candles are so dear? But we may thank our own luxury for these impositions. I see no reason why we should not humble these upstarts by making our own candles; aye, and our own bread too, as our forefathers have done before us.

The tallow-chandlers, to excuse themselves, lay the fault on the melters. The melters shift it from themselves to the butchers; and so the game goes round.

Oh but, say they, the government will lose part of its revenue: to which I answer, that rather than they shall raise candles to double their value, on pretence of paying a penny per pound excise; in case the parliament will take off the duty on candles for the ease of the poor, I will present them with a project gratis, which shall bring in almost double the money now levied by candles, and that without the least hardship on the subject.

Having, I hope, taken sufficient care of street-robbers, I proceed now to clear the roads from highwaymen, footpads, &c.

Let parties of horse be stationed at all the outgoings from the city of London; so that if a coach, wagon, &c., want a convoy, two, three, or more may be detached by the commanding officer; these shall be registered, and answerable for their charge; and for encouragement shall receive so much per mile, or in the whole, convoy money.

This may be likewise practised from town to town all over England, so that the roads will be as safe as the streets; and they who scruple the trifle of convoy money above proposed, merit not safety.

For those who walk on foot to the adjacent villages, parties of foot may be stationed in like manner; so that not only the subject will be free from danger, but the soldier employed and prevented from corrupt measures by this additional perquisite to his pay.

Nothing remains but that robbers be prosecuted at the public charge; the trials fixed to respective days, that prosecutors may not lose so much time, and the rewards paid in court without deduction or delay; nor should any robber be admitted an evidence after he is taken, or pardoned after conviction.

Daniel Defoe – A Short Biography

Daniel Foe was born around 1660 in Fore Street in the parish of St. Giles Cripplegate in London.

The aristocratic-sounding 'De' was added to his name to create 'Defoe'. On occasion he was prone to claim descent from the family of De Beau Faux.

His father, James Foe, was a prosperous tallow chandler and a member of the Worshipful Company of Butchers and, with Defoe's mother, Annie, Presbyterian dissenters.

Defoe has been born into a time that was rich in dramatic history. In 1665, 70,000 were killed by the Great Plague of London. The following year the Great Fire of London destroyed much of mediaeval London. The Defoe house was one of the few to survive.

In 1667, a third calamity beset London when a Dutch fleet sailed up the Medway via the River Thames and attacked the town of Chatham, as well as destroying much of the British fleet.

By the time Defoe was aged ten accounts suggest his mother, Annie, had died.

Defoe's education began at James Fisher's boarding school in Pixham Lane in Dorking, Surrey. By 14 he was attending a dissenting academy at Newington Green in London run by Charles Morton, and he is then believed to have attended the Newington Green Unitarian Church. During this period, the English government persecuted those who chose to worship outside the Church of England.

Defoe entered the world of business as a general merchant, dealing at different times in hosiery, general woollen goods and wine. His ambitions were great and he was able to buy a country estate, a ship as well as civets, though he was rarely out of debt. (The civet produces an odorous secretion for the purpose of marking out their territory. Diluted, after some time, the odor of civet secretion, normally strong and repulsive, becomes pleasant with animalistic-musk nuance. The animals are kept in cages in order to be able to collect the secretions and thence perfume).

In 1684, Defoe married Mary Tuffley, the daughter of a London merchant, and received a dowry of £3,700 – a huge amount by the standards of the day. With his debts and political difficulties, the marriage may have been troubled, but it lasted 50 years.

In 1685, Defoe joined the ill-fated Monmouth Rebellion but gained a pardon, by which he escaped the Bloody Assizes of the notorious Judge George Jeffreys.

The Glorious Revolution brought Queen Mary and her husband William III to the crown in 1688, and Defoe became one of William's close allies and a secret agent. Some of the new Government policies led to conflict with France, thus damaging many of Defoe's trade relationships.

In 1692, Defoe was arrested for debts of £700 and his civets were taken away. His actual debts are thought to have been nearer £17,000. His laments were loud and he always sided with debtors, but there is evidence that his financial dealings were always above board.

With a wife and seven children to support it was essential that his release was quickly enabled. He achieved this and accounts then suggest he travelled to Europe and Scotland, perhaps to re-establish some business relationships and to trade wine.

By 1695, he was back in England, serving as a "commissioner of the glass duty", and responsible for collecting the tax on bottles. The following year, 1696, he ran a tile and brick factory in what is now Tilbury in Essex and the family lived in the parish of Chadwell St Mary.

Defoe's first notable publication was not one of his great fiction works but a series of proposals for social and economic improvements, a subject for which he had a keen eye and many ideas. An Essay upon Projects was published in 1697.

His most successful poem, The True-Born Englishman (1701), defended the king against the perceived xenophobia of his enemies, satirising the English claim to racial purity. That same year Defoe presented the Legion's Memorial to the Speaker of the House of Commons and later his employer, Robert Harley, flanked by a guard of sixteen gentlemen of quality. It demanded the release of the Kentish petitioners, who had asked Parliament to support the king in an imminent war against France.

In 1702 the death of William III once more created a political crisis. Queen Anne immediately began an attack against Non-conformists. Defoe was one of the first targets. His pamphleteering and political activities quickly resulted in his arrest. This seemed mainly predicated on his December 1702 pamphlet; The Shortest-Way with the Dissenters; Or, Proposals for the Establishment of the Church, which argued for their extermination. In it, he ruthlessly satirised both the High church Tories and those Dissenters who hypocritically practised so-called "occasional conformity". Although it was published anonymously, the Defoe's authorship was quickly unmasked and he was arrested and charged with seditious libel. In fact, Defoe's ironic writing had been misinterpreted, but, alas for him, his trial was to be at the Old bailey in front of the sadistic judge Salathiel Lovell.

Lovell sentenced him to a punitive fine of 200 marks, to public humiliation in a pillory at Charing Cross and an indeterminate length of imprisonment at the Queen's pleasure which would cease only on payment of the enormous fine.

This was an awful moment for Defoe. After his three days in the pillory, he was imprisoned at Newgate.

In despair, he wrote to William Paterson, the London Scot and founder of the Bank of England and who was in the confidence of Robert Harley, 1st Earl of Oxford and Earl Mortimer, a leading minister and spymaster in the English Government. Harley arranged Defoe's release, in 1703, in exchange for Defoe's co-operation as an intelligence agent for the Tories. In exchange for such co-operation with the rival political side, Harley paid some of Defoe's very large outstanding debts, which greatly improved his financial situation.

With his release from Newgate Defoe had, within a few days, witnessed the Great Storm of November 26th, 1703. It caused immense damage to an area from London to Bristol, uprooting millions of trees, and claiming the lives of over 8,000 people, mostly at sea. This became the subject of The Storm (1704), which included many eye-witness accounts and is regarded as one of the world's first examples of modern journalism.

In the same year, he set up his periodical A Review of the Affairs of France which supported the Harley Ministry, and chronicled the events of the War of the Spanish Succession (1702–1714). The Review initially ran weekly but was soon being printed three times a week. Defoe wrote most of the articles himself and although in effect the Review was a Government publication Defoe was enthusiastic and energetic as ever.

Harley was ousted from the ministry in 1708, but Defoe continued writing the Review to support a new master, Godolphin, then again to support Harley and his return in the Tory ministry of 1710–1714. The Tories fell from power with the death of Queen Anne, but Defoe continued his work, now for the Whig government, writing 'Tory' pamphlets that undermined the Tory point of view.

Not all of Defoe's pamphlet writing was political. One pamphlet was originally published anonymously, entitled 'A True Relation of the Apparition of One Mrs. Veal the Next Day after her Death to One Mrs. Bargrave at Canterbury the 8th of September, 1705.' It deals with the crossover between the spiritual and physical realms and describes Mrs. Bargrave's encounter with her old friend Mrs. Veal after she had died.

In 1709, Defoe authored a rather lengthy book entitled The History of the Union of Great Britain. The book attempts to explain the facts leading up to the Act of Union 1707, dating all the way back to

December 6th, 1604 when King James was presented with a proposal for unification. (It should be remembered that since the death of Queen Elizabeth England and Scotland, although separate kingdoms, had a common monarch; known as James I of England and as James VI of Scotland. The act now brought the two countries into one; Great Britain.

Part of Defoe's duties as a Government spokesman and spy was the relaying of the Governments view to the public. He thought that his work on the Review would end the threat from the north and gain for the Treasury an "inexhaustible treasury of men", a valuable new market increasing the power of England, clearly the senior partner in the Union. In September 1706, Harley ordered Defoe to Edinburgh to do everything he could to secure loyalty to the Treaty of Union. Defoe was conscious of the risk he was taking. His reports were often vivid descriptions of violent demonstrations against the Union. "A Scots rabble is the worst of its kind", he reported.

Defoe was a Presbyterian who had suffered in England for his convictions, and as such he was accepted as an adviser to the General Assembly of the Church of Scotland and committees of the Parliament of Scotland with little problem.

Defoe received little in the way of reward or recognition from his pay-masters or the government. However, like any good writer, the experiences would be filed away for later use. The Scottish experience was helpful when he came to write his Tour Thro' the Whole Island of Great Britain, published in 1726.

Defoe continued to keep up a wide and varied output including in his apologia Appeal to Honour and Justice (1715), a defence of his part in Harley's Tory ministry (1710–14), The Family Instructor (1715), a conduct manual on religious duty; Minutes of the Negotiations of Monsr. Mesnager (1717), in which he impersonates Nicolas Mesnager, who negotiated the Treaty of Utrecht (1713); and A Continuation of the Letters Writ by a Turkish Spy (1718), a satire of European politics and religion, written by Defoe in the guise of a Muslim in Paris.

From this point Defoe would now enter a period of writing that would cement his place in the canon of English fiction. From 1719 to 1724, Defoe published the novels for which he is now world-famous including Robinson Crusoe in 1719 and Moll Flanders in 1724 amongst many others.

In the final decade of his life, he also wrote conduct manuals, including Religious Courtship (1722), The Complete English Tradesman (1726) and The New Family Instructor (1727).

Defoe seemed to have a natural knack of writing across a wide range of subjects and from a number of points of view. He published on the breakdown of the social order; The Great Law of Subordination Considered (1724) and Everybody's Business is Nobody's Business (1725), together with works on the supernatural; The Political History of the Devil (1726), A System of Magick (1727) and An Essay on the History and Reality of Apparitions (1727). His works on foreign travel and trade include A General History of Discoveries and Improvements (1727) and Atlas Maritimus and Commercialis (1728). Perhaps his greatest achievement is the magisterial A Tour Thro' the Whole Island of Great Britain (1724–27), which provided a panoramic survey of British trade on the eve of the Industrial Revolution.

Published in 1726, The Complete English Tradesman is a late example of Defoe's political and social work. He discusses the role of the tradesman in England in comparison to those abroad, arguing that the

British system of trade is far superior. He also states that trade is the backbone of the British economy: "estate's a pond, but trade's a spring."

Defoe was obviously keenly aware of both political and economic structures. Trade, Defoe argues, is a much better vehicle for social and economic change than war. He states that through imperialism and trade expansion the British empire is able to "increase commerce at home" through job creation and increased consumption. This increased consumption, by laws of supply and demand, increases production which in turn raises wages for the poor therefore lifting part of British society further out of poverty.

Daniel Defoe died on April 24th, 1731. Some accounts say that it was whilst hiding from his creditors. Indeed, Defoe was known to enjoy walking on a Sunday when, legally, it was the only day of the week when he could not be legally pestered about his bills. The cause of his death was given as lethargy, but it is thought it was more probably a stroke.

He was interred in Bunhill Fields, London. A monument was erected to his memory there in 1870.

There are various suggestions as to the number of works in Defoe's literary output. Certainly, no less than 200 separate pieces but accounts suggest perhaps as many as 500 which seems, even for so prolific a writer as Defoe, rather too generous but perhaps is in keeping with the extravagance of his life.

Daniel Defoe – A Concise Bibliography

Defoe wrote an immense amount of works. Some were under pseudonyms or anonymously and others may merely have been attributed to him. The list below is by no means exhaustive but is certainly illustrative of both his range and scope.

Novels
Robinson Crusoe (1719)
The Farther Adventures of Robinson Crusoe (1719)
Serious Reflections During the Life and Surprising Adventures of Robinson Crusoe; With His Vision of the Angelic World (1720)
Captain Singleton (1720)
Memoirs of a Cavalier (1720)
A Journal of the Plague Year (1722)
Colonel Jack (1722)
Moll Flanders (1722)
Roxana: The Fortunate Mistress (1724)
Memoirs of a Cavalier: A Military Journal of the Wars in Germany, and the Wars in England.: From the Year 1632 to the Year 1648 (1724)
A New Voyage Round the World (1725)
Military Memoirs of Capt. George Carleton (1728)
A General History of the Pyrates, From their First Rise and Settlement in the Island of Providence, to the Present Time (1724)
The History of the Pyrates (1728)
Of Captain Misson and his Crew (1728)

Essays, Satires & Other Pieces

An Essay Upon Projects (1697)
The Shortest Way with the Dissenters (1702)
New Test of Church of England's Loyalty (1702)
Ode to the Athenian Society (1703)
Enquiry into Acgill's General Translation (1703)
The Storm– a description of the worst storm to hit Britain in recorded times, which includes eyewitness accounts. (1704)
The Great Law of Subordination Consider'd (1704)
Layman's Sermon on the Late Storm (1704)
Elegy on Author of 'True–Born Englishman,' (1704)
Hymn to Victory (1704)
An Essay on the Regulation of the Press (1704)
Giving Alms No Charity (1704)
The Consolidator or, Memoirs of Sundry Transactions from the World in the Moon (1705)
A True Relation of the Apparition of Mrs. Veal (1706)
Sermon on the Filling-up of Dr. Burgess's Meeting-house (1706)
History of the Union of Great Britain (1709)
Atalantis Major (1711)
A Short narrative of the Life and Actions of His Grace John, Duke of Marlborough (1711)
A Seasonable Warning and Caution Against the Insinuations of Papists and Jacobites in Favour of the Pretender (1712)
Short Enquiry into a Late Duel (1713)
A General History of Trade (1713)
An Answer to a Question That Nobody Thinks of, VIZ. But What if the Queen should die? (1713)
Reasons Against the Succession of the House of Hanover with an Enquiry How far the Abdication of King James, Supposing it to be Legal, Ought to Affect the Person of the Pretender (1713)
Wars of Charles III. (1715)
The Family Instructor (1715)
Hymn to the Mob (1715)
The Family Instructor (1715)
An Appeal to Honour and Justice, Though It Be of His Worst Enemies: Being A True Account of His Conduct in Public Affairs (1715)
A Friendly Epistle by Way of Reproof from one of the People Called Quakers, to T. B., a Dealer in Many Words (1715)
Memoirs of the Church of Scotland (1717)
Life and Death of Count Patkul (1717)
Memoirs of the Church of Scotland (1717)
Memoirs of Major Alexander Ramkins (1718)
Memoirs of Duke of Shrewsbury (1718)
Memoirs of Daniel Williams (1718)
A Vindication of the Press (1718)
Dickory Cronke: The Dumb Philosopher: or, Great Britain's Wonder (1719)
The King of Pirates (Capt. Avery) (1719)
Life of Baron de Goertz (1719)
Life and Adventures of Duncan Campbell (1720)

Mr. Campbell's Pacquet (1720)
The Supernatural Philosopher; or, The Mysteries of Magick (1720)
Due Preparations for the Plague (1722)
Life of Cartouche (1722)
Religious Courtship (1722)
History of Peter the Great (1723)
The Highland Rogue (Rob Roy) (1723)
Narrative of Murders at Calais (1724)
The History of The Remarkable Life of John Sheppard (1724)
A Narrative of All The Robberies, Escapes, &c. of John Sheppard (1724)
A Tour Thro' the Whole Island of Great Britain, Divided into Circuits or Journies (1724–1727)
The Great Law of Subordination; or, the Insolence and Insufferable Behaviour of Servants in England (1724)
Account of Jonathan Wild (1725)
Account of John Gow (1725)
Every-body's Business, Is No-body's Business (1725)
The Complete English Tradesman (1725; volume II, 1727)
The Friendly Demon (1726)
Mere Nature Delineated (Peter the Wild Boy) (1726)
Essay upon Literature and the Original of Letters (1726)
History of Discoveries (1726–7)
A System of Magic (1726)
The Protestant Monastery (1726)
The Political History of the Devil (1726)
An Essay Upon Literature (1726)
Mere Nature Delineated (1726)
Conjugal Lewdness (1727)
Treatise concerning Use and Abuse of Marriage (1727)
Secrets of Invisible World Discovered; or, History and Reality of Apparitions (1727)
Parochial Tyranny (1727)
A New Family Instructor (1728)
Augusta Triumphans: or, The Way to Make London the Most Flourishing City in the Universe (1728)
Plan of English Commerce (1728)
Second Thoughts are Best (on Street Robberies) (1728)
Street Robberies Considered (1728)
A Plan of the English Commerce (1728)
Humble Proposal to People of England for Increase of Trade, &c. (1729)
Preface to R. Dodsley's Poem 'Servitude' (1729)
Effectual Scheme for Preventing Street Robberies (1731)

Works in Verse
A New Discovery of an Old Intreague (1691)
Character of Dr. Samuel Annesley (1697)
The Pacificator (1700)
The True-Born Englishman: A Satyr (1701)
Reformation of Manners (1702)
The Mock Mourners (1702)

More Reformation (1703)
Hymn to the Pillory (1703)
The Dyet of Poland (1705)
Jure Divino. A Satyr in 12 books. (1706)
Caledonia (1706)
Translation of Du Fresnoy's "Compleat Art of Painting" (1720)

www.ingramcontent.com/pod-product-compliance
Lightning Source LLC
Chambersburg PA
CBHW072358190626
46811CB00019B/1400

* 9 7 8 1 7 8 7 3 7 4 3 2 4 *